D0419254

PHIL REDMOND'S
BROOKSIDE
— LIFE IN THE CLOSE —

by Geoff Tibballs

**A CHANNEL
FOUR BOOK**

B⊕XTREE

Acknowledgements

The author and publishers would like to thank the following
for their kind assistance in the preparation of this book:
Phil Redmond, Mal Young, Philip Reevell, Janice Troup, Helen
Griffin, Alexis Redmond as well as the staff and cast of *Brookside*
at Mersey Television and Chris Worwood at Channel Four stills.

First published in Great Britain in 1994 by Boxtree Limited

3 5 7 9 10 8 6 4 2

Designed by Blackjacks, London
Printed and bound in Glasgow by Bath Press Colour Books

Boxtree Limited
Broadwall House
21 Broadwall
London   SE1 9PL

A CIP catalogue entry for this book is available
from the British Library.

ISBN 1 85283 946 5

number 5

For Sheila Grant, it was a dream come true – her own home in the smart new development called Brookside Close. It would all be so different from the run-down council estate where she and Bobby, her husband of 24 years, had struggled to raise their three kids, Barry, Karen and Damon. That estate was only a mile away but it could have been the other side of the world. No longer would she have to worry about gangs roaming the streets at night or languish in an area where the only gainful employment went to the council workers who boarded up the residents' windows. Deprivation and violence did not go hand in hand with home ownership. A devout Catholic, Sheila had worked hard to make a decent life for herself and her family. Now she had the chance to taste the fruits of her endeavours.

Bobby was not so sure about the move. True, he liked the prospect of a better house but the principle of home-ownership clashed head-on with his own principles as a committed socialist and trade unionist. He somehow felt he was betraying the working-classes. A big bear of a man, he told his workmates at Fairbanks Engineering that Sheila had made him move. There was an element of truth in that but Bobby was by no means as unwilling a participant as he made out. For the bottom line was that he was proud of being able to give Sheila what she wanted for once.

The oldest of the Grant offspring was Barry. To all intents and purposes, he was Bobby's boy although it later emerged that his real father was Matty Nolan. By November 1982, Barry was in his mid-twenties yet showed no desire to settle down either with a girl or a job, although he was a joiner by trade. Barry did not like to conform. He was a rebel with only one cause – himself. Working in a factory held no interest for him. He preferred to indulge in his own money-making schemes, most of which operated on just the wrong side of the law. Sheila had an inkling of what he was up to but chose to turn a blind eye. She doted on him and he in turn would defend his 'mam' against anybody. That included Bobby. For when mother and son are that close, there is invariably friction with the father. Oedipus never had much time for his dad either. With Barry and Bobby, communication was at a premium and when they did talk, it invariably ended in a slanging match. Barry couldn't understand why the man he took to be his father was so obsessed with unions and politics. Bobby couldn't understand why his son had no beliefs and was such a layabout. But he suspected that the real reason Barry had no convictions was simply because the police hadn't caught up with him yet.

Karen and Damon were typical teenagers but with markedly different prospects. She was bright and pretty with a college future beckoning. He was a 'scally' – a cheeky, well-meaning lad who found school work a bore. His idea of a good read was a Liverpool Football Club programme. His one clear-cut ambition was to leave school as soon as possible.

At that stage, Damon had no time for romance. He devoted his energies to playing truant and mucking around with his mates Ducksie Brown and Gizzmo Hawkins. Together, they were the terrors of the Close, poking fun at Alan Partridge and playing tricks on Paul Collins whose officious manner made him a natural target. Karen, on the other hand, had no shortage of admirers. One of the first was 'Demon' Duane who saw the fact that Karen was on the Pill as a passport to sleeping with her. Matters came to a head at his flat. He accused her of being a 'teaser'. It looked as if he was about to rape her but instead he threw her out into the cold November night air. On the way home she met Barry who, acting out his role as big brother, went round and left both Duane and his cherished Honda motorbike in a heap. Karen's next suitor was Jeff Bacon until she gave him the cold shoulder.

Sheila soon found that life on the Close was not all a bed of roses. Within a couple of months of their moving in, number 5, along with every other house, was burgled. To make matters worse, Sheila and Bobby were under-insured. Bobby brought home his work problems too. He had been at Fairbanks for nigh on 25 years and, as foreman and shop steward, now decided to mobilise the troops into strike action in protest at management. Sheila found herself in an awkward situation. Not only did she have to contend with Bobby's moods at home, but at the baker's where she worked she began to feel the wrath of customers whose husbands were on strike and who blamed Bobby for the whole mess.

Sheila was feeling the strain. She rounded on Karen for going to a party instead of Midnight Mass and, on finding a card of contraceptive pills in her daughter's bedroom, accused her of sleeping around. Karen revealed that their doctor had put her on the Pill to combat her period pains, an issue which she had not been able to discuss with the unsympathetic Sheila. What's more, Karen insisted that she was still a virgin.

The situation at Fairbanks worsened throughout 1983 and, with Sheila being made redundant and Barry being sacked from his job after he and pal Terry Sullivan were caught stealing building materials, the atmosphere at number 5 was decidedly tense. When rumours about the factory's impending closure became fact, Bobby too faced redundancy, not an appealing prospect for a man in his late forties with the millstone of a mortgage hanging around his neck. The purse strings were tightened. Sheila had been promised a new sofa but had to settle for new seat covers instead. Nevertheless it was a sacrifice she was willing to make. She urged Bobby to fight the closure and, taking a leaf out of her husband's book, even organised the wives into a Women's Action Group. The wives pleaded the case on television but it was all in vain. In November, Fairbanks closed.

Bobby was devastated. A man had a right to work. Without a job, he wasn't a man. He loafed around the house, brooding. Sometimes he didn't even bother getting out of bed. Against his wishes, Sheila set up a non-registered employment agency. She

asked him to do a job for the agency but he had more interesting fish to fry – talking to union man George Williams about the possibility of standing for a full-time union post. Not wanting to let Sheila down, Matty Nolan, Bobby's friend and former workmate from Fairbanks, offered to do the agency job instead. As he left number 5 with his toolbox, he was stopped and accused of fraud by an officer from the DHSS.

Things began to look up for Bobby. The commitment he had shown to the union during the strike enabled him to be elected District Secretary. He was back on his feet. The swagger returned. He had always known that the union wouldn't let him down. When he had been drawing the dole, he had been forced to sell his old Austin Princess to make ends meet. Now he had a brand new Austin Montego, courtesy of the union. By way of celebration, he and Sheila went on holiday to Spain.

Barry continued to sail close to the wind, conducting an affair with Irene Harrison, the sex-starved wife of his amateur football team manager, before taking a shine to the newly-widowed Petra Taylor across the Close at number 10. Women came and went but Terry, his friend since school, was always there for him. Together, they came up with more get-rich-quick schemes. They created a stink when trying to sell some dodgy perfume in a pub. When a warning about the stuff was broadcast on the radio, they made an instant business decision and offered to clean the pub with the perfume in exchange for drinks. They tried car valeting and a tool-hire business but made the mistake of becoming involved with a video enterprise run by local villain Tommy McArdle. When Bobby learned about Barry's crooked sideline, he wasted no time in throwing him out of the house. It was the excuse he had been waiting for.

Before long, Bobby had more on his mind than a wayward son. While on holiday in Spain, Sheila plucked up the courage to announce that she was pregnant. She had known before they went but hoped that a couple of weeks in the sun might soften him up. To her immense relief, he was delighted. But then she never could predict Bobby's reaction to anything. Just when the rest of the family were getting used to the news, Karen's latest boyfriend Andrew roared into the Close on his motorbike. He failed to spot Sheila in time and sent her crashing to the tarmac. Luckily, no real harm was done.

In January 1985, Claire Grant entered the turbulent world of Brookside Close. Sheila became depressed after the birth but just when she needed Bobby's support, he immersed himself in union business, conducting meetings in the lounge. It may have been minutes to him but for her it seemed like hours. Bobby was never one for half-measures. If he accidentally chipped the skirting-board, he'd more than likely redecorate the whole house. So his answer to Sheila's post-natal depression was to have a vasectomy. Discovering that he couldn't get it done on the NHS without Sheila's consent and knowing full well that her Catholic beliefs would never condone such a drastic move, he sneaked off and had the operation done privately. One day, he arrived home, sore and groggy. Sheila was alarmed, all the more so when an attempt to climb a ladder left him doubled up in pain. She demanded the truth. Bobby confessed. Her concern erupted into fury. She accused him of political hypocrisy in going private and of going against the Church. In disgust, she moved into Claire's room.

> *'They don't care. They just want 12 months out of you, then they couldn't care less. I worked like mad for them. I worked days I didn't have to, I worked overtime and I didn't get a penny for it, cos I wanted a job.'*
> – Damon Grant on being released from the YTS scheme

By now, Barry had decided to seek fame and fortune in London. The last straw was a beating-up at the hands of Tommy McArdle after Barry had tried to help George Jackson's defence in the warehouse robbery case by withdrawing his support for the alibi of McArdle's henchman, Victor. McArdle was not a man to cross. There was no hiding place from him in Liverpool. He seemed to control everything. Barry half expected him to be wearing the number seven shirt at Anfield one week.

Karen meanwhile had started at Liverpool University, taking a course in communication studies. She threw herself into university life, getting to work on the students' newspaper and middle-class Guy Willis with equal enthusiasm. She began staying out at night and, after more false starts than the 1993 Grand National, she finally lost her virginity.

Naturally, Damon's progress was less spectacular. On leaving school, he joined a YTS scheme with a painting and decorating firm. He enjoyed the work – even though he was suspended after being wrongly accused of stealing a vase – and believed the promises of a 'proper job' when the scheme ended. It was not to be. He was sent packing with nothing more than a standard letter of reference to make way for the next intake. Damon lost what little faith he had left in human nature.

Sheila and Bobby achieved a degree of reconciliation. But things would never really be the same again. His love affair with the union blossomed, putting all other relationships in the shade. Desperate to find a way out of her daily drudgery, Sheila enrolled in a further education course on local history and managed to persuade the despairing Matty, still unemployed after the closure of Fairbanks, to do the same. Bobby, never a likely role model for 'new man', couldn't understand why Sheila should want anything more from life than the honour of cooking his meals and darning his socks. His mistrust developed into jealousy when he suspected Sheila of having an affair with tutor Alun Jones. Bobby resented the fact that they seemed to be operating on a higher intellectual level than him. But then sometimes the good folk of *Trumpton* operated on a higher intellectual level than Bobby Grant.

Jones was certainly smitten with Sheila but the feelings were not returned. She just enjoyed the opportunity of having somebody interesting to talk to for a change. However, Matty did not hold back and fell for the dubious charms of divorcee Mo Francis. Matty's affair brought a fresh crisis to the Grant household. Bobby stubbornly refused to believe that Matty was capable of seeing another woman while Sheila agonised over whether to tell Matty's wife, Teresa. Sheila tried to separate Matty and Mo but, for her pains, received threatening letters from Mo and abuse from Matty. But eventually Sheila's message got through and Mo gave Matty the elbow.

One evening in July 1986, Sheila was lured to The Swan by Alun Jones on the pretext of discussing the course. Suddenly she realised he was making a pass at her. She tried to escape. Matty, drowning his sorrows, saw the struggle and started ranting and raving about how Sheila Grant, the woman who wrecked his relationship, was at it herself. Sheila stormed out of the pub, pursued by both men. She hailed a taxi, only for Matty to jump in beside her. She sat there terrified while he continued his tirade. Finally she could take no more. As the cab reached a quiet lane near the Close, she leapt out and set about walking the rest of the way home. She had gone no more than 100 yards when she heard someone call out her name. Before she could react, a coat was thrown over her head and she was raped in a clump of bushes.

Neighbour Pat Hancock was the first suspect since he had fresh scratch marks on his face. Then Matty and Alun Jones were questioned. Ultimately, the taxi driver was charged and convicted. But it was all too late for Teresa Nolan. Matty had told her about the affair with Mo and, on hearing that a man had been charged with Sheila's rape, Teresa assumed that it was Matty. Seemingly with nothing to live for, she jumped off a ferry into the Mersey . . .

For months, Sheila had nightmares about her ordeal. Bobby did his best to understand what she was going through but it could never be enough. Barry, back on one of his regular visits to stay one step ahead of the law, dealt with it in the only manner he knew how – he buried the hatchet with (instead of in) Tommy McArdle and got him to have the rapist beaten up.

Karen had moved into a cramped bedsit with Guy but found him increasingly possessive. So she upped and left to further her education in London, but only after making sure that Sheila would be able to cope without her. For mother and daughter had become much closer of late, initially through a shared interest in studying and then in the aftermath of the rape.

Encouraged by Father Gibbons, Sheila decided that a trip to Rome would speed the recovery process following her ordeal. Bobby, who was more concerned about an asbestos problem at Billinge Chemicals, said they couldn't afford to go. Sheila maintained that she had a spiritual need and, if necessary, would go on her own. To pay for it, she got a part-time job at The Swan. Bobby was livid. When Matty tried to persuade him to accompany Sheila to Rome, Bobby flew off the handle, saying that everybody saw her point of view rather than his own. Nobody considered his feelings. Damon became so fed up with his parents' childish bickering that he threatened to leave home. It

seemed to knock some sense into the pair of them and, albeit reluctantly, Bobby agreed to make the pilgrimage to Rome. After a sticky start, when old resentments resurfaced, they came to an understanding, realising that, beneath the tension, they still loved one another. But, like Rome, the Grants' marriage could not be re-built in a day.

Meanwhile, Damon had been starting to show a healthy interest in the opposite sex. Gail, a keener home-builder than Wimpey, was replaced before she could get him up the aisle by young Debbie McGrath. For Damon, Debbie was the real thing. But her father did not approve and marched round to number 5 to tell Damon to leave Debbie alone. Even Sheila and Bobby had to concede that Debbie was a bit young. Damon was convinced that the real problem lay with the fact that he hadn't got a job. He rectified the situation, doing door-to-door sales. It was a hopeless cause. So he packed it in. Back to square one. Then Mr McGrath

Barry Grant contemplates the error of his ways.

A grieving Sheila Grant at son Damon's funeral.

made him an offer he couldn't refuse – a job in Ipswich. Damon said he would take the job but vowed that it wouldn't have the desired effect. He would continue seeing Debbie. Returning from Ipswich, Damon learned that Debbie's mother had left home and that the atmosphere with her father was tense. He noticed a bruise on Debbie's neck. She passed it off as a sporting injury but eventually confessed that her father had hit her. This was too much for Damon. He got Debbie to pack her bags. The two young lovers quit Liverpool.

Sheila was saddened. She felt that she and Bobby had let them down. A month later, she was grief-stricken. She and Bobby were just about to go out when a policeman knocked on the door. Damon had been stabbed to death in York.

At the funeral service, the priest described Damon's life in glowing terms but Barry stepped in to put the record straight. Predictably, Bobby strongly voiced his disapproval of Barry's actions but, equally predictably, Sheila backed her favourite son to the hilt.

When the news had sunk in, Sheila found herself drawn closer to Debbie. They had both loved and lost Damon. Bobby, on the other hand, wanted someone to blame. He chose Debbie. The result was that he and Sheila began to drift even further apart.

Bobby started to hit the bottle and lost his driving licence after being caught drinking and driving. He and Barry argued yet again. Barry left. Sheila accused Bobby of forcing him out. Most conversations in the Grant household now required a referee. At Matty's suggestion, Bobby made an attempt to be nicer to Sheila but she buried her head in her Open University books. He noticed that the lounge looked a bit tatty and secretly got the decorators in. He reckoned Sheila would be pleased but instead she was cross because the new decor had removed all traces of Damon's own handiwork. Bobby hadn't thought.

In an effort to breathe life into their ailing marriage, they went out for a meal but found they had little to talk about. Back home, Bobby mistook Sheila's need for emotional closeness and forced himself on her. Sheila's mind was in a turmoil. She even followed a boy home, thinking it was Damon.

Barry learned that Debbie was pregnant. Her father wanted her to have an abortion but Sheila would not hear of it even though Debbie was diabetic and the baby could be deformed. Barry had to throw Mr McGrath out of the house after he had insulted the memory of Damon. Later, Bobby heard that Debbie had suffered a miscarriage. As it turned out, he was misinformed.

Seeing her relationship with Bobby crumbling before her eyes, Sheila went to see a marriage guidance counsellor. Bobby meanwhile was worried about a different union. Without telling Sheila, he put his wages into a strike fund to support the apprentices at Bishop and Wardle who were faced with losing their jobs. When she found out, there was another blazing row which he countered by demanding to know why she hadn't told him about the visit to marriage guidance.

The crunch was not long in coming. Sheila's friend Kathy Roach persuaded her to go to a nightclub. It would do her good, get her from under Bobby's size 11s. But Bobby was a bear with a sore head. He didn't want his wife going clubbing and flatly refused to look after Claire. He stormed out of the house, thinking that it would therefore be impossible for Sheila to go anywhere. However, Sheila was determined. She was not going to let Bobby ruin a rare chance of having fun, of actually putting a smile back on her face. So a bemused Billy Corkhill was roped in to look after Claire at number 10. While Kathy and Sheila were out enjoying themselves, Bobby returned home to an empty house. Furious, he threw a suitcase full of Sheila's things onto the Close and then beat a path over to the Corkhills' to reclaim Claire, smashing Billy's front door in the process. Eventually, Sheila and Kathy arrived back, followed by two men they had met at the club. Hearing the commotion, Bobby went over to investigate. The men quickly departed and Bobby slapped Sheila around the face. She was humiliated.

At Sheila's request, Barry fixed the Corkhills' front door but Bobby promptly argued with Billy and broke it again. It seemed as if a door war was about to break out when Billy announced his intentions of smashing the Grants' door but Kathy managed to restrain him. Bobby admitted that the reason for his concern about the apprentices was a feeling of guilt over Damon. It was too late for talking, though. A few days later, Bobby walked out – never to return. Sheila took Claire away to Basingstoke for a while and put the house up for sale. The house which six years earlier had seemed to be the answer to her prayers, now held too many unhappy memories.

It was all very well selling the house but Sheila still needed a roof over her head. Kathy persuaded Billy to let Sheila and Claire stay at number 10 and in September 1988, they formally moved into the Corkhills' extension.

Sheila may have lost Damon and Bobby but she still had Barry. The number one son decided that a few readies – no matter how they were earned – might come in handy for his 'mam'. So he ran a few errands for the sinister Sizzler, a stuttering villain who made Barry an offer he couldn't understand. First, Barry seduced the glamorous Penny Riozzi at a designated hotel room. No sooner had they finished than Sizzler entered waving a video of their activities. Rarely had *coitus* been so rudely *interruptus*. Sizzler used it to blackmail Penny as a means of gaining control of her husband Franco's betting shops. But Barry strayed from the script by taking a shine to Penny. In order to get the video-tape back, he had to do another job for Sizzler – persuade a tough old boot by the name of Ma Johnson to hand over her gaming arcade to Sizzler's organisation. Ma was more than a match for Barry so Sizzler ordered him to kill Ma's dog and deliver its head to her. That way, she might just change her mind. Barry wasn't blessed with too many scruples but even he drew the line at killing a dog.

A potential buyer was soon found for the Grants' house but then fate intervened in the shape of Tracy Corkhill's slovenly boyfriend Jamie Henderson. Abandoning the habits of a lifetime by doing a day's work, Jamie indulged in a spot of window-cleaning during the course of which he succeeded in breaking the Collinses' sink. In a hare-brained attempt to cover his tracks, he replaced their bathroom suite with the one from the Grants' empty house. So when Barry returned to number 5 and switched the water back on, the bathroom was flooded. Not surprisingly, the sale fell through along with the floorboards.

Jimmy 'No Fixed Abode' Corkhill seized the opportunity to squat there for a while but when the house was boarded up, he had to break out – something of a change for Jimmy who has always been more used to breaking into houses. As the state of the house began to deteriorate and with no likely buyers on the horizon, it was decided to put it up for auction.

Two doors along, at number 7, Frank Rogers was agonising over the house they had recently purchased from Harry Cross and whether it was big enough for the whole family. Purely out of curiosity, he went along to the auction of 5 Brookside Close but mid-way through, found himself gripped by auction fever and ended up buying the Grants' old house at a knock-down price. So in May 1989, Frank and his family made the short move along the Close.

Long-distance lorry driver Frank had been married to Chrissy for 16 years. Their backgrounds were quite different. Frank's was tinged with sadness, his father having been tortured and killed by the Japanese during the War. Frank wasn't one to wear his heart on his sleeve but it was clear that, as a boy, he had missed having a dad around. Frank was a working-class hero through and through. He liked a drink with his mates and expected Chrissy to be around to look after the kids and the house. A woman's place was in the home. Like Bobby Grant, Frank's attitudes were positively neanderthal. And, like Sheila Grant, Chrissy Rogers occasionally wanted something more from life. She was intelligent and articulate. The only articulate thing about Frank was his lorry. As a student in the late Sixties, she had the world at her feet but then she met Frank and quickly fell pregnant with Sammy. Her dreams vanished in a haze of Nappisan. She knew she was too young to get married but felt that she had little choice. Besides, Frank did have his good points. He was fun to be with, a natural performer, a legacy of his days with Liverpool band The Scotty Dogs. They may have been overshadowed in the Merseybeat era by The Beatles, The Searchers, Gerry and the Pacemakers, Billy J. Kramer *et al* but The Scotty Dogs still had their moments. *Nobody Butters The Toast Like You* remained a minor classic. Frank enjoyed nothing more than a nostalgic trip down memory lane. He even still had his old Sixties Cortina, immaculately maintained in its original maroon and a guitar strap given to him by Billy J. Kramer. Chrissy preferred not to hark back. There were too many might-have-beens.

But Chrissy still wanted to change the world in her own small way. Because she cared. Oh how she cared. Sometimes she cared so much, it hurt. Sometimes her caring bordered on interference. Frank, on the other hand, wasn't a thinker. He might think about what he would like for tea but that was about as far as it went. But he was a loving father, albeit with an alarming tendency to fly off the handle. (He had been convicted for actual bodily harm in the Sixties.) And he was a loyal husband. He would never consider straying. His idea of a bit on the side was an extra portion of chips.

Their eldest daughter, Sammy, was confident and attractive with no shortage of boyfriends. Frank thought the world of her. Younger sister Katie was much quieter, more introverted. She acquired her intensity from her mother. But it was their brother Geoff, commonly known as 'Growler', who was

Frank's real pride and joy. Frank had always wanted a professional footballer as a son and, no sooner had they moved into number 5, than Geoff was invited for a trial with Tranmere Rovers. Frank was thrilled but Chrissy was decidedly less enthusiastic. For Geoff had been diagnosed as dyslexic and Chrissy thought that his education was far more important than kicking a ball around. She pointed out the risks of a footballing career but Frank wouldn't listen. As far as he was concerned, she was being a killjoy.

Chrissy continued to campaign for her son's rights to a proper education. Her efforts, decried by Frank, resulted in Geoff receiving specialist tuition from a peripatetic teacher. Frank was more concerned with the boy's feelings – he was being singled out at school – and tried to ease the pain by presenting him with a new bike. He suspected Chrissy's motives for the campaign, believing that she was doing it for herself, rather than Geoff.

Despite the short distance, the move was not the smoothest of operations. The children argued over bedrooms and even when agreement was reached, Katie was scared of spending the first night on her own and crept in to share with Sammy. Frank and Chrissy were horrified to find the bathroom infested with dry rot. Frank arranged for a workmate, Lennie, to repair it for £500. As with most of Frank's ideas for getting things done on the cheap, it backfired. The rot set in. They didn't get their money back and instead finished up with a bill for £2,000. Meanwhile, the resourceful Sammy staged a decorating party in her room. But there was an unwanted outcome when she fell out with boyfriend Owen Daniels after catching him flirting with her best friend, Nisha Batra. They were soon reconciled.

To the embarrassment of her family, Chrissy became a vociferous member of the Parent-Teachers' Association at Brookside Comprehensive. One day, Katie was kept in late at school to pick up litter, principally because Chrissy had complained about the state of the school at a recent PTA meeting. Chrissy was furious to discover that Katie had been given an essay to write as punishment for being cheeky and made her pen an explanation for her actions. For Katie, home had become a second school. Frank was convinced that Katie's problems in class all stemmed from Chrissy's involvement with the PTA. To him, membership of the Conservative Party would have been more acceptable. His moans fell on deaf ears.

The Rogers' kids – our Sammy, our Geoff and our Katie.

Chrissy announced that she would stand as a school governor.

When it was something he was interested in, Frank was capable of interfering just as much as Chrissy. Learning that Geoff was being picked on by a bigger boy at Tranmere, Frank demanded that the coach take action. Geoff was mortified.

The relationship between Sammy and Owen was anything but smooth. She wanted to enjoy herself – with other lads if necessary – while he revealed a jealous streak. When she came back from a holiday in Italy, he was angry to see a number of photos of a local romeo called Luigi. Later he made a scene after catching Sammy and her friends Nisha and Ronnie being dropped off by Kav and Tony, two lads they had met at a club. The following week, Owen reluctantly agreed to join the five on an evening out. He was immediately suspicious of the car the lads were driving, strongly believing it to be stolen. He didn't want to get in but Sammy persuaded him. The police spotted the car and gave chase. Owen's worst fears were confirmed when Tony blurted out the car was stolen and so they couldn't stop. The chase hotted up. Sirens wailed. Tyres screeched. Then the stolen car veered off the road at high speed and crashed. Kav and Tony were killed, Nisha and Ronnie suffered concussion and Sammy and Owen lay in comas. Sammy quickly came out of hers but, on hearing the seriousness of Owen's condition, she was racked with guilt. It was her fault Owen had got into the car. Why hadn't she listened when he said he thought it was stolen?

Owen came out of his coma but remained in hospital. Sammy took it badly. First she turned to cider before moving on to gin. On one hospital visit, she was so drunk that Chrissy was summoned to collect her. As the worst baby-sitter since Richard III, Sammy was meant to look after little Jessica Choi at number 7, but paid greater attention to the drinks cabinet. When Michael Choi returned, sozzled Sammy argued bitterly with his scientist girlfriend Alison Gregory over animal rights. To make her point, Sammy paint-sprayed the word 'murderer' along the side of Alison's car.

Frank found himself the innocent pawn in an NCT management plan to close down the maintenance department and put the work out to tender. His colleagues blamed him for the threat to their jobs. Pricked by his conscience, he joined the workers' co-operative, very much against the wishes of Chrissy who stipulated that his family responsibilities had to take priority. At the same time, he was told that he was in line for the post of Assistant Transport Manager. He didn't tell Chrissy. Sure enough, the co-op won the tender and Frank was offered the desk job, something Chrissy had been constantly urging him to work towards. No more days and nights away from home, travelling the length and breadth of the country in a cramped lorry cab. At last the chance to be a proper family. But when it came to the choice, Frank felt compelled to turn it down, unable to leave the workers in the lurch. He just dreaded Chrissy finding out.

Katie had problems of her own. She was being bullied at school by a girl called Bagga who tried to force her to steal money. She confided in Geoff and he and his pal Bumper Humphries endeavoured to sort out Bagga and her gang. But to no avail. To avoid a beating-up, Katie stole some loose change from Chrissy. Eventually, Katie plucked up the courage to tell her mother everything. Chrissy provided a shoulder

Frank Rogers head-butts the father of Paula Heneghen, Geoff's girlfriend. Mr Heneghen disapproved of the relationship – he didn't think the Rogers were good enough for his daughter.

no.5

1

It was a big day, not only for Sammy, but for the whole Rogers family.

2

Everyone was busy toasting the happy couple, unaware of the drama that was unfolding upstairs.

The Exit of Chrissy Rogers

Chrissy Rogers could stand no more. The last straw was the way in which husband Frank had bulldozed Owen Daniels into marrying their pregnant daughter Sammy. But then Frank always was a union man. Chrissy couldn't bear to watch history repeating itself, so she decided to leave, timing her departure to coincide with Sammy and Owen's wedding day on 8 November 1991. It was a present neither wanted.

So while the reception was in full swing downstairs, Chrissy was quietly packing her bags in the bedroom. She hoped to sneak out unnoticed but came face-to-face with young Katie. Despite Katie's pleas, Chrissy was determined to go and walked out of the Close to start a new life.

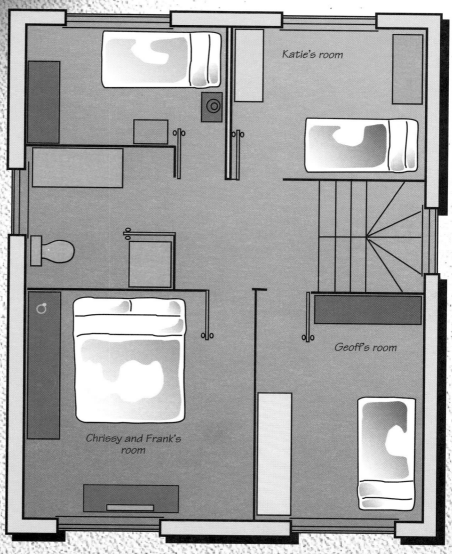

Katie's room

Before her departure, Chrissy removed her wedding ring and placed it on the bedside table.

Chrissy and Frank's room

Geoff's room

A distraught Katie peered through the bedroom window, watching her mum walk out.

to cry on. She did not want another daughter going off the rails.

Chrissy remained desperately worried about Sammy's drinking. Frank was not much help. His answer to everything was to shout. She booked Sammy in to see Dr O'Rourke. He was sympathetic, he listened. Chrissy struck up an instant rapport with him. When Chrissy got home and started quoting the doctor at him, Frank lost his temper. He mistrusted experts in any field. Surely there was a bloke at work who could have cured Sammy's drink problem for a few packets of fags . . .

As the weeks went by, Chrissy found herself confiding more and more in Joe O'Rourke. When Sammy, petrified that she might have helped to put Owen in a wheelchair for the rest of his life, drank herself into a stupor and wet her bed one night, the doctor understood. Given the lack of support she felt she was receiving from Frank, the inevitable happened. Chrissy was drawn closer to Dr O'Rourke.

'Frank, you've got to come out of the Stone Age.'

– Chrissy Rogers

Fearing that the workers were cutting corners, Frank packed in the co-op but his boss, Marsland, refused to give him his old job back. Much as she resented Frank joining the co-op in the first place, Chrissy was just as annoyed that he had left it. Without a regular income, she said, they would lose the house. Frank seemed incapable of making a sensible decision.

Money was too tight to mention. Soon everybody in the house seemed to be looking for a job. Sick of school but drying out, Sammy successfully applied for a chambermaid's job in a Blackpool hotel; Chrissy, after being made redundant from the estate agent's where she worked, considered a receptionist's post at Dr O'Rourke's surgery; and Frank, having seemed preoccupied with river pollution in the wake of an incident involving Katie, got a job as Assistant Transport Manager with LICHEM, only to lose it owing to unsatisfactory

references. Two months later, he landed another lorry-driving job. Meanwhile, to the horror of Geoff and Katie, Chrissy became the new school secretary.

By then, Sammy and Owen had little in common. She treated him like dirt. Now that he could walk again, her guilt was eased. Finally, after openly flirting with the newly-arrived Mike Dixon, she dropped Owen. He wandered around like a lost labrador. Free at last, Sammy wasted no time in finding a replacement – her boss at the hotel, Tim Darby, a divorced man of 39. Chrissy and Frank were united for once in their condemnation.

On a rare night out with her old student friend Gina, Chrissy expressed the fear that Sammy would be trapped into settling down too soon – just like she had been. Chrissy had been forced into marriage with Frank because she was pregnant. She told Gina about the near-affair with Joe O'Rourke who had made her feel young and reckless again. Later, Frank accidentally overheard Chrissy saying she regretted not having pursued a teaching career and attacked her for being selfish. He said she should be worrying about her daughter's future, not her own past. Only Frank was allowed to reminisce.

In March 1991, Sammy left home and moved in with Tim. Fresh from headbutting the father of Geoff's girlfriend, Paula, Frank again showed his diplomacy by storming round to the hotel and demanding his daughter back. He warned Tim that if he broke Sammy's heart, he'd break him! It soon became apparent that Tim was none too comfortable with having Sammy living in. She was too immature. He'd had his bit of fun, but now he had tired of her. Following an awkward dinner with his grown-up children, Chloe and Adam, Sammy learned that Tim was going

Trying to be reasonable for once, Frank endeavours to explain his feelings to Sammy's lover, Tim Derby.

away for three weeks. A month later, on her 18th birthday, he finished with her. She was hysterical and refused to go so he drove her back to the Close and dumped her things on the pavement. Sammy was not giving up without a fight. She went back to Tim's house and caused a commotion on the doorstep. He threw a bowl of water over her. Most girls would have got the message by now, but not Sammy. She tried telling him she was pregnant. He called her bluff. So, in a last-ditch effort to win back his affections, she hurled a brick through his window. This was courtship Rogers-style. Her dad would have been proud of her.

Against all the odds, Owen was waiting to cushion Sammy's fall from grace. She didn't deserve him. Brother Geoff had also been shown the door, by Tranmere. Disillusioned, he walked out of his school exams but quickly landed on his feet with a YTS placement at Torquay United.

The writing was on the wall for Chrissy and Frank. They could scarcely agree about anything. She hated the way he had allowed himself to get into a rut and told him it was time he faced reality. The argument ended with her telling him about Dr O'Rourke. She assured him that nothing physical had happened but Frank didn't want to know and kicked her out. Frank turned on Sammy and blamed her for the break-up of his marriage. Everybody was in the wrong but him. Chrissy and Katie stayed with Gina for a few days before, driven by Katie's unhappiness, Chrissy agreed to a tearful reunion with Frank.

It was only a brief respite. The following month, Sammy announced that she was pregnant by Owen and that they were going to get married as soon as possible. Frank was pleased that Owen was doing the right thing by his daughter but Chrissy was appalled. All she could see was Sammy making the same mistakes as she had nearly 20 years earlier. She was throwing her life away. She tried to talk them out of getting married, which led to more raging rows with Frank. Chrissy knew the situation was hopeless. She and Frank were not even on the same planet. She had to get out before it was too late. She handed in her notice at the school, telling the new deputy headmistress, Barbara Harrison, that she had got a place at teacher training college.

Frank remained blissfully oblivious to it all. He went out with Owen on his stag night and offered his advice on how to manage a successful marriage. It was like the captain of the Titanic giving a lecture on ship safety. When they got back, Chrissy quietly told Owen that it was still not too late to back out but his mind was just about made up. To cut costs, the wedding reception was held at the Rogers' house and so, as Frank dispensed *bonhomie* downstairs and made his fatherly speech, upstairs Chrissy was preparing to leave him. She took off her wedding ring, placed it on the bedside table and walked out into the Close with her cases, watched from an upstairs window by a tearful Katie. Another marriage had bitten the dust at number 5.

It didn't take Frank long to adjust to life without Chrissy. After all, he'd never really noticed her much when she had been there. His main concern was that Owen should get a job, support his new family the way a man should. This led to a clash with Owen's parents who wanted him to go back to college. Education was a sore point with Frank.

On 5 June 1992, baby Louise was born. Owen's new job selling conservatories (a marked improvement after serving pizzas) kept him away from the birth and contributed to Sammy's feelings of depression. Beset by money troubles and unable to cope with being a mother, Sammy rejected the baby and abandoned her in her pram outside the hospital maternity unit. Owen took Louise to his mum's and announced that he was getting a divorce. Sammy didn't seem to care. Frank found himself in the unlikely role of mediator and finally succeeded in

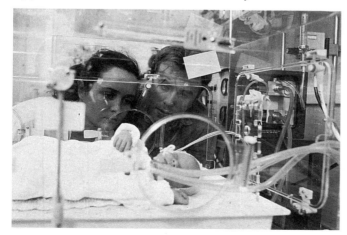

Sammy and Owen anxiously monitor the progress of baby Louise.

no.5

1

Barry tried all manner of threats to force Simon and the cult to vacate the house.

3

Simon moved his bomb from the garage into the lounge. He thought they had 30 minutes to escape but timing wasn't his strong point.

4

The explosion rocked Brookside, blowing out windows all over the Close.

The Cult Kidnap Barry Grant

When Simon Howe and his dotty disciples adopted 5 Brookside Close as their church, the residents were quickly up in arms. It seemed that the cult's days were numbered when Barry Grant bought his old family home but, to Barry's frustration, they showed no sign of moving. Rather than wait for the law to take its course, Barry took the matter into his own hands and, as a one-man SAS team, he stormed the place with a gun.

Overpowered, he was tied up and held hostage in Geoff Rogers' old bedroom where he was subjected to hideous red wallpaper, tuna sandwiches and the gospel according to St Simon. With the bailiffs imminent and increasing concern regarding Barry's whereabouts, Simon packed all but Terry off to Bristol and produced a home-made bomb. The plan was to free Barry and destroy the house but the bomb went off too soon. Ironically, it was Simon who suffered the most serious injuries.

upstairs

2 Simon soon found that it would be easier to convert the loft than convert Barry.

getting Sammy and Owen talking again. They decided to try again. The most important thing was to find a little place of their own.

By then, Frank had taken up with Lyn, the sister of a workmate who had been killed in a lorry crash while doing a favour for Frank. The biggest threat to their relationship was Lyn's man-eating sister Bev who had already slept with Lyn's first husband, Steve, and was soon taking an unhealthy interest in Frank. Fortunately, Ron Dixon took Bev off his hands by never taking *his* hands off Bev. If Frank's blood pressure had been spared the strain of a fling with Bev, maybe the very thought of it had weakened him. For in the autumn of 1993, he suffered a minor heart attack while driving. Lying in hospital, he told Lyn that the shock had made him realise what was important in life. He proposed to her and she didn't hesitate in accepting.

The only blot on the horizon was Lyn's teenage daughter Alison who was less than enthusiastic about the forthcoming nuptials. She gave the impression that she would rather have had Hannibal Lecter for a step-father. Frank also faced pre-wedding problems from his own kids. Geoff returned from Torquay, ostensibly because the reserves didn't have a game. But it emerged that Geoff had walked out, dejected because he couldn't even get into Torquay United Reserves. He could not admit to his dad that

he was a failure – he knew how much his footballing career meant to Frank.

In time, Alison came round and the wedding day dawned with Frank surrounded by his families – old and new. In celebration, he knocked back the champagne. After the Register Office ceremony, Lyn arranged for Frank to drive her in the Rolls-Royce to the reception. Frank was thrilled and young Tony Dixon tagged along for the ride after falling out with his father. Frank took them on a little detour, straight towards a car driven by drug-crazed Jimmy Corkhill. Frank swerved violently, the Rolls went out of control and smashed into a wall. Lyn was slightly injured, Tony Dixon lay in a coma and Frank was killed. What with Chrissy walking out when Sammy tied the knot, Frank didn't have much luck with wedding days.

The repercussions began. Katie blamed Lyn for allowing Frank to drink and drive, particularly with his heart condition. Seeking comfort, Katie turned to the deeply religious Simon Howe who worked at the garage. She found that talking to Simon helped and was pleased when he asked her out. Meanwhile, Chrissy turned up and expressed surprise at Lyn's declaration that she was going to continue living in the house. Chrissy thought that Frank would have wanted the house to go to his own children. The crisis escalated when Sammy

Smiles before the tragedy on Frank and Lyn's wedding day. Little did they know that Frank would never get to cut the cake.

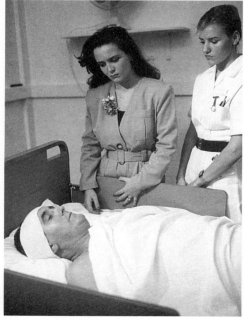

The end is nigh for Frank Rogers.

Lyn and Sammy fight over Frank's cherished guitar.

and Owen moved in. There simply wasn't enough room for both sets of children. Sammy behaved particularly spitefully. She and Lyn struggled over Frank's old guitar. Lyn lost her footing and tumbled down the stairs, losing the baby she was carrying. Frank's baby. Suitably ashamed, Sammy retreated with Owen to their flat. Lyn decided to put the house up for sale.

> *'The forces of darkness have declared war on us and we must not be found wanting.'*
> – Simon Howe addressing his disciples

Katie Rogers had always been impressionable. She had an unfortunate taste in friends. Remember teenage temptress Leanne Powell? Now Katie was smitten with Simon. He initiated her into his religious family and soon controlled her mind and actions. The cult began to hold their meetings at number 5 and Simon moved in with Katie. It was God's will. Even Terry Sullivan, an agnostic if ever there was one, found himself trapped in Simon's web and, in order to look the part, grew a Manson-like beard. When Simon ordered Katie to sleep with Terry, she began to see through her mentor. She refused and ran out, seeking refuge with Jacqui Dixon at number 8. Poor Katie thus found herself evicted from her dad's old house – Simon and the group had moved in as squatters and showed no inclination to move. Simon urged Terry to buy the house on behalf of the cult but, before they could

act, a 'Sold' sign went up. Barry Grant had purchased it.

Barry wanted Simon out but the Chosen One was determined to stay put. Barry's impatience was finally exhausted when Simon started preaching outside Barry's nightclub, La Luz, about the perils of drinking and partying. In his inimitable way, Barry decided to take things into his own hands. Armed with a gun, he tried to break into the house with the intention of kicking the cult out on to the street. However, he was overpowered, pinned down and held hostage in Geoff Rogers' old bedroom. Everyone on the Close thought Barry had done one of his familiar runners or even gone bankrupt, little knowing that he was being held captive across the road.

Simon, unsure of his next move, sent his followers to spread the word in Bristol. Terry remained. Eventually, Simon decided that if they couldn't have the house, no one could. He made a bomb and, releasing Barry just before impact, planned to send chunks of number 5 into orbit. All the windows on the Close were smashed to pieces but the damage to number 5 was only superficial. Simon was no better at making bombs than at spreading God's word.

Barry, as usual came out shaken, but not stirred, and Terry suffered minor injuries but Simon's life hung in the balance before he began to make a steady recovery, Terry constantly by his side. The damage gave Barry the chance to have the place done up – all leather sofas and chrome – and he moved in, amid much gossip, with Penny Crosbie. As he reclined in Sheila and Bobby's old bedroom, with Lady Penelope by his side, he wondered what his 'mam' would think of him now. Many boxes of Kleenex later, 5 Brookside Close was back in the Grant family.

Katie falls under the religious spell of Simon Howe.

number 6

The bungalow at 6 Brookside Close remained unoccupied until April 1983. It had visitors all the same, in the shape of Damon Grant and his partners-in-crime, Ducksie and Gizzmo, who used it as a den of iniquity.

The arrival of the new owner, burly Alan Partridge, put an end to their tenancy although they continued to take a keen interest in his lifestyle. Alan worked as a freelance computer programmer. He was a born enthusiast, whether it was playing rugby or talking at length about the joys of computers, a topic guaranteed to break the ice at parties. He was the sort of chap on whom even the Samaritans would hang up.

However, there was no denying that he was good at his job – so good, in fact, that he had been advised to spend some of his hard-earned cash before the taxman got his hands on it. Acting accordingly, he had moved out of his mother's house and bought number 6. With him came all manner of paraphernalia (computer software, old engine parts, a boat) most of which he stored under a tarpaulin at the side of the bungalow. He later enhanced the rear of the property by constructing a typically eccentric Japanese garden. There weren't too many of those in Brookside Close. But Damon and his gang were more interested in another of his appendages – someone called Sam. Not unreasonably, they assumed Sam to be male and concluded that Alan must be gay. They were in for a pleasant surprise when Sam turned out to be short for Samantha, a blonde-haired, leggy ex-model. The boys could only dream. Ducksie entered uncharted territory by washing behind his ears.

Alan had met her at a computer fair – she was a systems demonstrator – and had relentlessly pursued her ever since. He wanted to get married but she was quite happy with the way things were. Nonetheless, she did agree to move in with him. For Alan, it was a step in the right direction. He persisted with his proposals, calculating that by the law of averages, she must eventually say 'yes'. After weeks of constant badgering, she did indeed succumb, after a fashion. They agreed to have a competition to see who could earn the most money over the next three months. If Alan won, Sam would get engaged. A lost contract scuppered Alan's chances but, to his delight, when they returned from a skiing holiday, she asked him to marry her. He promptly ran out onto the Close, screaming for joy. Larger than life was our Alan.

They settled on a Register Office wedding but first Sam had to move out of the bungalow and back into her flat to accommodate Alan's domineering mother. He did not want her thinking that he and Sam had been living in sin. On the build-up to the big day, Sam received a number of phone calls from her agent offering her the job of a lifetime in Los Angeles. She turned it down, on the grounds that she was getting married, but it set her thinking. Alan had more pressing problems. On the day of the wedding, his best man let him down and, in the absence of a suitable replacement, he was forced to accept Paul Collins' offer to deputise. In the end, he had no need of a best man. Late arriving for the ceremony, Sam was on the brink of 'pledging her troth' when she suddenly had a change of heart and ran out. It was a terrible shame – all those vol-au-vents going to waste.

When he had recovered from the initial shock, Alan desperately wanted to make contact with Sam to find out what had caused her change of heart. She thought she owed him an explanation too and so they

Marcia gives her answer to Sinbad's proposal at Goodison Park.

got together. She told him that although she loved him, she couldn't marry him at the moment. Sam said goodbye, leaving Alan deeply hurt.

Increasingly lonely, he became the victim of a spot of matchmaking when Harry Cross tried to pair him off with Heather Huntington. To Heather's relief, Alan assured her that he had no designs on her. Instead he began seeing Liz, a former girl-friend, until they fell out in spectacular fashion. Alan had been accused of plagia-rism after trying to sell Gordon Collins' computer programme on his behalf. Wounded to the core, Alan proceeded to get extremely drunk and lurched out onto the Close, hurling abuse at the neighbours. A couple of days later, he learned from Heather that Liz was responsible for the misunderstanding over the programme. End of relationship.

Alan continued to drift along aimlessly until Gordon Collins tipped him off that Sam was working at the International Garden Festival. Although he again made a spectacle of himself by hitting the booze, Sam took pity on him and they both realised that they were happier together than apart. When Alan received the offer of a lucrative job in Kuwait, the pair decided to sell up and get married. In July 1984, Sam finally became Mrs Partridge and the newlyweds left Liverpool and 6 Brookside Close.

Next door at number 7, something was stirring. Harry Cross had devoted his life to the railways. At 18, he had worked in the sheds at Edge Hill, graduating to every boy's dream of fully-fledged train driver in his forties. He was one of the old school, a man who had always done an honest day's work for an honest day's pay. He had no time for slackers, shirkers or indeed anyone who didn't agree with his views. If his mind had got any narrower, his head would surely have come to a point. The one thing you could say in his favour was that he treated everyone with the same disdain. Young and old, regal and humble, they all came alike to Crossy. Grumpy, petty, spiteful, stingy – Harry could have re-cast the Seven Dwarfs. When he retired, he took his lump sum, his British Rail pension and his long-suffering wife Edna and bought 7 Brookside Close, in a quiet cul-de-sac in which to spend their twilight years. Although his heart appeared to be made of granite, it was medically-speaking weak.

Harry was determined that it should not be subjected to any unnecessary strain which basically meant getting Edna and anyone else within earshot to run around after him. The biggest mystery was how she never took an axe to him in his sleep.

Shortly after meeting up with old friends Ralph and Grace Hardwick, Harry suffered a minor heart attack at the city's International Garden Festival. His doctor told him to take things easy and advised Edna and son Kevin to bring Harry's bed downstairs. Now Harry had a genuine medical excuse for getting people to wait on him hand and foot. He wallowed in his condition. But he thought the novelty of sleeping downstairs on his own might soon wear off and – although he didn't care to show it too often – he was very fond of Edna. He missed her. So, hearing of Alan Partridge's impending departure, he came up with a plan. He would buy the bungalow and rent out number 7 to suitable tenants, if any such species existed in Harry's world. Thus in September 1984, Harry and Edna became the new owners of 6 Brookside Close.

As Harry saw it, the great advantage of a landlord living in such close proximity to the rented property was the considerable scope it afforded for snooping. Net curtains had a life of their own when Harry was around. Before letting his acquisition, Harry prepared a questionnaire to test out prospective tenants. He asked Edna to fill it in. She got a very low score. Harry wondered what he was married to. The first likely tenants were two young nurses, Kate Moses and Sandra Maghie. Harry liked the look of them. Not only might they be able to cure his back pains but they paid the rent in advance. They told him that there would be a third tenant, Pat. Harry could hardly wait to meet the girl.

It was Edna who discovered that Pat Hancock was a muscular male hospital porter. Mischievously, she refrained from telling Harry. She wanted him to find out for himself. When he did, he was predictably disapproving. Two girls living with a man under the same roof – his roof. He felt he had been tricked.

In November 1984, Grace Hardwick died. Although Ralph was an old colleague of Harry's on the railways, it was to Edna that he was particularly close. They shared the same sense of humour. Harry had none to share. Ralph was suitably distraught at Grace 's death and was not relishing the prospect of living alone. Edna felt sorry for him and persuaded Harry to let him move in with them.

Harry hoped that Ralph might be able to stop Edna's gambling. She had always liked a secret flutter on the horses but things were beginning to get out of hand. He kept finding betting slips in her handbag. But Ralph's solution was to suggest that Edna should open a credit account at the book-maker's. What with that and Ralph's desire to redecorate the lounge the moment he had moved in, Harry was beginning to wonder what he'd let himself in for with this *ménage-à-trois*.

On one of her gambling expeditions, Edna won a sizeable sum on a six-horse accumulator but Tattersall's the book-makers, an outfit run by Tommy McArdle, refused to cough up. Harry had always been vociferous in his opposition to betting on horses but here, with his own financial gain at stake, he decided to make an exception. He helped Edna wage war against Tattersall's, daubing slogans outside the shop and writing to *The Sporting Life*. McArdle was so unnerved by the campaign that he offered Harry a settlement of £4,000. Without consulting Edna, he immediately accepted.

Not long afterwards, Edna was mugged while returning from the Post Office after collecting her pension. Although not seriously hurt, she was badly shaken. As the weeks went by, she became increasingly housebound. A large basket of fruit arrived with a note from Tommy McArdle telling her that the mugger had been dealt with. Then one day while Harry was nosing about next door, Edna collapsed in the kitchen. The chip pan caught fire. When Harry returned, he panicked and ran for help. Fortunately, Terry Sullivan was on hand to deal with the blaze. Edna had suffered a stroke. She couldn't speak.

Harry wasn't ready for this. They were supposed to enjoy a long and happy retirement together. Now he had to face the prospect that he might lose her. He realised how much he loved her, how he couldn't live without her. For once, he appeared almost human. He refused to put her in a geriatric ward and, with no other bed available, kept her at home. When Sandra called round to see if there was anything she could do to help, Harry vented his frustrations with the National Health Service on her. Realising he had gone too far, he apologised. Apologies did not come easily to Harry Cross but these were extenuating circumstances.

Despite Harry's attentive nursing, Edna suffered a relapse. There was no alternative but to move her into hospital. Still she failed to respond. On 3 September 1985, she passed away. At the funeral, the vicar mistook Ralph for Edna's husband. It all added to Harry's grief.

The kindly Ralph helped Harry's rehabilitation and suggested a railway holiday in Wales where they enjoyed a ride on the foot-plate of a steam train on the famous Blaenau Ffestiniog railway. It was something Harry had always wanted to do. They also bought a gaudy pink Fiesta at an auction. Ralph could already drive but Harry's attempts to learn were doomed to failure. He could only drive on rails.

Sinbad: *'I've done my bit. A fresh turkey, free range, as promised. All you've got to do is pay me the balance. A fiver, and it's yours to kill.'*

Harry: *'Do you think you can get an old soldier with that one? Ralph, get the carving knife out!'*

Back at the Close, Harry and Ralph decided to decorate the bungalow for Christmas in memory of Edna. With his usual eye for a bargain, Harry agreed to buy a cut-price turkey off Sinbad but when Sinbad turned up on his doorstep, the turkey, christened 'Trevor', was still very much alive. Harry called Sinbad's bluff and it was much to Sinbad's relief when 'Trevor' re-emerged from the bungalow unscathed. All in all, Harry didn't have much luck with his purchases that Christmas since he and Ralph ended up buying the same present for each other.

Five months had passed since Edna's death and Harry began to think about female companionship. Ralph was a good friend but he had his limitations. For a start, he didn't look too hot in high heels. Convinced that Edna would not have minded, Harry set about penning an advert in the personal columns. Ralph backed him all the way, hoping for someone else to bear the burden that was Harry, but even his patience was exhausted over preparing the advert. No one would be able to come up to Harry's high standards. Yet amazingly, Harry received a number of replies. By far the most promising was from Madge Richmond, a respectable lady from the Wirral. They arranged to meet at the Walker Art Gallery and Ralph tagged along to give his considered opinion. Waiting for the rendezvous, Harry panicked and approached the wrong woman who let him know exactly what she thought of him. In the meantime, Ralph had made contact with the real Madge – and they were getting along famously.

Harry proved particularly difficult over the coming weeks. He resented the way Madge seeming to be coming between him and Ralph. So when Ralph wanted to tart himself up for a rendezvous with the belle of Birkenhead, Harry deliberately spent as much time as possible in the bathroom. Ralph was swept off his feet. Soon he and Madge were planning a holiday in Torquay. Harry said he'd go too – he had never heard of playing gooseberry. This left Ralph with little option but to fix him up with a partner. Harry had set his sights on Heather but had to lower them considerably to take in Julia Brogan, the woman with a mouth the size of the entrance to the Mersey Tunnel. Harry had to make the best of a bad job.

Back in Liverpool, he received a rare visit from son Kevin and his partner Sally Haynes. Harry had always disapproved of the relationship because they were not married but now that she was about to make him a grandad, the old animosity began to fade. Harry went over the top, buying huge teddy bears for the baby, and planning to install Kevin and Sally in number 7, once he had got rid of Pat

Sinbad's scheme to sell live turkeys for Christmas was not one of his more successful enterprises.

Hancock and Terry Sullivan. However Sally had no desire to move in next door and told him so. Harry lost his temper and Sally went into labour. The baby, little Harriet, was born prematurely. Full of remorse, Harry begged her to survive but his prayers were not answered. The baby died. Harry was plunged into grief for the second time in just over a year.

He sensed that Ralph might also be coming to grief over Madge. There was something about her which wasn't quite right. She seemed too good to be true. Even Harry struggled to find fault with her. His suspicions were aroused when Madge rang Ralph to say that it was her birthday the following day. Harry clearly recalled her previously announcing that it was on a different date altogether but when he confronted her about her two birthdays, she told him he must have been confused. He warned Ralph to keep an eye on her. But in Ralph's case, love was blind. The Darby and Joan duo went on holiday to Spain in February 1987 and returned engaged. Harry couldn't believe that Ralph could be so easily taken in, particularly when it emerged that owing to a mix-up over travellers' cheques, Madge had no money in Spain, leaving Ralph to pay for everything. That, of course, included the expensive-looking engagement ring which she flourished under Harry's nose.

Harry was now more convinced than ever that Madge was a gold-digger. A sneak look at her driving licence confirmed that he was right about her two birthdays and when Julia Brogan remembered seeing Madge outside the Art Gallery with another man and a second lonelyhearts ad of his own brought a reply from Madge, Harry decided to go undercover. Disguising his voice and using an assumed name, he arranged to meet her. She turned up. Her story was blown. Under fierce interrogation,

she confessed that there were six other Ralphs. Harry made her promise to call off the wedding. The next day, Madge called round to end the engagement. She told Ralph a cock-and-bull story about still grieving for her dead husband. Ralph tried unsuccessfully to get her to change her mind. As she departed, Harry made her leave the engagement ring behind.

Ralph was shattered, and accused Harry of splitting them up out of sheer spite. For once in his life, Harry kept quiet – even when Ralph packed his bags to leave. But on his way out of the Close, he was collared by Julia Brogan who told him the truth. Realising that he had misjudged his old mate, he promptly returned to number 6.

Reunited, Harry and Ralph began to ponder their mortality. Julia, who was never reluctant to impart advice, told Harry he should use his money to enjoy the rest of his life and so he decided to sell number 7 in order that he could live for today. But after buying Pat and Terry out, Harry continued to play landlord, renting the house to the Rogers. The moment Frank's articulated lorry pulled up, he took an instant dislike to them.

Harry had always relished the thought of a position of authority where he could throw his weight around and be generally awkward. The opportunity arose when he was appointed doorman at the local Commonwealth and Empire Club. On his first day in the job, Ralph tried to join and Harry took great pleasure in ejecting him. Few bouncers were more malicious than Harry Cross. Thumbing through his bible, the club rule book, Harry did find a rule which would allow Ralph entry but, once inside, he was not permitted to buy a drink or join in any of the club's activities. And the chances of him being bought a drink by Harry were remote to say the least. Ralph's membership hung in the balance and Harry, generous as ever, saw the chance to blackmail him by suggesting that failure to obey Harry's every desire around the house could seriously jeopardise Ralph's chances of joining the club. Ralph was finally accepted but Harry still had one more trick up his sleeve. When both applied for the coveted post of Entertainment and Concert Secretary and Ralph looked like winning, Harry uncovered an obscure club rule which forced Ralph to withdraw. His joy was short-lived. As Harry gave his inaugural speech, which was against women being allowed to join, Councillor Redfearn died and the Third Light Rule took effect. This meant the whole committee had to be re-elected. It was left to Ralph to book the entertainment for Commonwealth Day.

Alas, it transpired that he had hired a male stripper! It was about as suitable as booking a juggler for a radio show. Luckily, Julia saved the day by singing, and club secretary Arthur Parkinson revealed that both Harry and Ralph had been elected to the committee.

In November 1988, Harry finally sold number 7 which left him free to concentrate on more pleasurable pursuits such as Arthur Parkinson's widowed sister Betty and the news that he would be a grandfather after all. Kevin's Sally was pregnant again. The Scrooge-like Harry even dressed up as Father Christmas – albeit reluctantly – and bought 30 cuddly seals off Sinbad. But Ralph had to have his dog Rommel put to sleep after it had chewed one of Harry's seals. Realising the seals were more toxic than cuddly, Harry headed for the club and snatched them back from the children. That was more like the Harry they knew! Overall, however, Christmas 1988 was a good one for Harry since he was called away from the club to go to the hospital where he held his new grandson Tim.

Harry never forgot Edna. They had been too close for too long. So it meant a lot to him when Sally allowed him to take little Tim to Edna's grave. Whenever Harry met Sally, there was still a feeling of tension, which sometimes exploded into a full-blown row, but generally they had come to accept each other. It never occurred to Harry that perhaps the one reason Sally didn't want to marry Kevin was the prospect of acquiring Harry as a father-in-law. Anyway, Harry had other matters on his mind when, on arriving at the cemetery, he was unable to locate Edna's grave. As it emerged that an entire section of the cemetery was being moved, Harry became hysterical. They couldn't just move his dear wife without telling him. He was yet more upset to learn that his so-called friend, Arthur Parkinson, had been commissioned to move the cemetery. Finding no support around the Close, Harry was left feeling sad and lonely.

He soon regained his fighting spirit and, after sending letters to the Queen and 10 Downing Street, set about the public humiliation of Arthur Parkinson by parading outside the Commonwealth and Empire Club wearing a sandwich board proclaiming Arthur to be a grave-robber. The war was resolved when Ralph took Harry to Edna's new grave, set in a tranquil spot. Harry agreed to drop his campaign.

A visitor to the Close in August 1989 was to have a profound effect on Harry's future. Her name was Lana Costello, an American

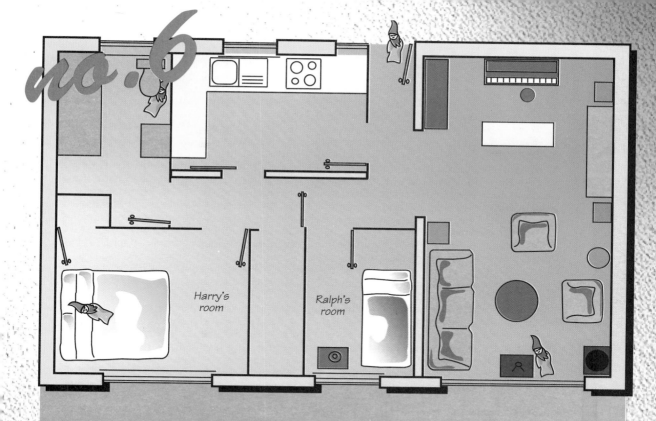

Harry's room

Ralph's room

Harry Cross' Gnomes

Harry Cross' collection of garden gnomes had always held a curious fascination for the children of Brookside Close. In the past, the Jackson boys from number 10 had taken great delight in relocating the little fellows up trees and when Mick Johnson moved into the bungalow as Harry's lodger, the gnomes again proved irresistible, this time to Mick's young son Leo. In the spring of 1990, Harry was away in Las Vegas acting as best man at Ralph and Lana's wedding. In his absence, Leo and Gemma came to stay with their father. The mischievous Leo proceeded to scatter the gnomes far and wide so that when the unsuspecting Mr Cross returned, he found that most of them had gone AWOL. Matters came to a head when he discovered a gnome in his bed – even Harry wasn't that fond of them.

friend of Gerald and Mona Fallon. For Ralph, it was Madge Mark II. He fell head over heels for Lana, immediately offering to show her the sights of Liverpool. At the time, Harry was away convalescing and was less than pleased to return and find a strange woman staying in the bungalow. Harry wanted Lana out and got his wish sooner than he expected when she announced that she was going to stay with Mona for a month. Ralph was invited too. Feeling lonely again, Harry let it be known that he was looking for a short-term lodger. Terry suggested his cab-driving mate Mick Johnson.

Mick was one of the few people on this earth who actually got on well with Harry Cross. What's more, the feeling was mutual so that when Mick informed Harry that he'd found himself a flat and would be leaving the following day, Harry played the invalid. Mick decided to stay. He was still there when Ralph and Lana returned. Ralph was forced to sleep on the couch as Harry was determined to prevent any funny business with Lana. Possibly remembering Madge or maybe because he dreaded being left alone, Harry did not take to Lana. He did everything he could to make life unpleasant for her, finally telling her that Ralph was only after her money. But lightning was not about to strike twice. Harry was powerless to wreck this relationship. Ralph asked Lana to marry him. She accepted and announced that they would be living back home – in Las Vegas. Apart from his pet dog Monty, Harry would be alone again, naturally.

When Ralph learned that Harry had tried to turn Lana against him, he was furious. The two old friends refused to speak. It was a sad sight. Lana tried to act as peacemaker but the pair were as stubborn as each other. All those years of living with Harry had obviously started to rub off on Ralph. The day of their departure dawned. Ralph began to mellow. He desperately wanted Harry to say goodbye but Harry refused. Ralph and Lana left Brookside Close. It was too late now. Whilst looking forward to his life with Lana, Ralph was bitterly upset that years of friendship with Harry should end in such a way. He was still looking over his shoulder – hoping – when they boarded the train at Lime Street. Suddenly, with better timing than the cavalry in a John Wayne film, Harry appeared. He had swallowed his pride and had come to say goodbye after all. Ralph was deeply moved. Arriving back home, Harry discussed his future with Monty. The pair of them decided to give Mick the chance to stay for good.

Mick came and went over the ensuing months but agreed to be around to look after Monty when Harry was invited to be best man at Ralph and Lana's wedding in Las Vegas. Given his feelings about gambling, it was a wonder Harry didn't try to close down every casino in Las Vegas. He did score an important point before leaving, however. When nobody in the Close seemed interested in his impending visit to the States, a vengeful Harry told the Council that the Corkhills' satellite dish hadn't got planning permission. And he did it in Paul Collins's name. It was a case of killing two birds with one stone – that would teach the Corkhills and the Collinses not to invite him round for Christmas dinner. Billy Corkhill went looking for the supergrass and a guilt-ridden Harry bought the dish off him for £50. To his dismay, he could only get racing fixtures on it – not a Betty Grable film in sight. So he sold it to Sinbad for £30.

Before Harry left, Mick took the opportunity to ask whether he could have his children, Leo and Gemma, round to visit. Big-hearted Harry immediately added a premium of £2 per week and compiled a list of kids' 'do's and don'ts'. As a document, it was only marginally shorter than the Magna Carta.

With Harry out of the way, Leo and Gemma popped round. They were living with their mum Josie. She and Mick were separated. Mick was a gentle giant, kind, considerate and steady, the sort of man most women would die for. Not Josie. She was very fiery and very Welsh. She wanted to party all the time, particularly with younger men who could bolster her ego, and had taken off with a sleazy medallion-man called Tony. Although she had two kids by Mick, she had yet to adjust to her responsibilities. Quite simply, she hadn't grown up.

Mick adored Leo and Gemma and couldn't wait for their visit. But it so nearly started in tragedy. While he went to sort out dinner, Mick left the children enthralled by Harry's goldfish pond in the back garden.

Happy families: Mick Johnson with Gemma and Leo.

Next door, Frank and Geoff Rogers were playing football. The ball accidentally went into Harry's garden and when Geoff went to retrieve it, he found Gemma lying face down in the pond. He screamed for help and began giving artificial respiration to the apparently lifeless Gemma. Geoff's quick-thinking – something for which he had never been noted at school – saved the day. Gemma recovered. Mick immediately filled the pond in with rubble. The accident left him with a mixture of bitterness and guilt. The bitterness was directed at Josie. He had tried to let her know what had happened but she had been out on the town. Typical.

Harry had always been very fond of his garden gnomes even though the inane fixed grins on their faces were totally at odds with his own personality. Somehow a stone hangman would have been more appropriate for his rockery. Unfortunately for Harry, Leo also took a shine to the gnomes and began redistributing them around the Close.

Mick was finding it hard work baby-sitting two kids and a dog. Something had to give. It was Monty. In frustration, Mick threw the little terrier out of the house. Monty took the hint – he knew when he wasn't wanted. Like his owner, he went into a major sulk and disappeared. Mick and the kids were beside themselves. Harry would go spare! They drew a 'wanted' poster to go on the side of Mick's taxi cab and set food in a trap. But all they managed to snare was a tiny kitten. The kids wanted to keep that too. Things were going from bad to worse, especially when the kitten vanished behind the dashboard of the car. Mick was forced to dismantle the vehicle, only for the kitten then to turn up. With Harry on his way home, two lads returned Monty. At least, it looked like Monty. But the dog seemed to think its name was Harry.

The homecoming of Harry was an episode in Mick's life that he would prefer to forget. When Harry woke up to find a gnome in his bed, Mick knew that it would be downhill from there. Sure enough, gnomes were missing and broken, ornaments rearranged, the pond destroyed and – worst of all for Harry – his beloved 'Monty' bit him on the nose! Harry was prepared to put it down to the fact that the dog had missed him until, that is, 'Monty' gave birth to pups. It was patently not Harry's dog.

> 'Get lost, Josie. I'm sick of you crying on my shoulder.'
>
> – Mick Johnson

In the late summer of 1990, Harry Cross left the Close to live in St Helens. Mick stayed on in the bungalow as Harry's tenant. Before long, Josie was visiting. She was having a rough time with Tony and seemed to be trying to edge her way back into Mick's life. For his part, Mick was still clearly physically attracted to her. He was putty in her manipulative hands – and she knew it. So when she announced that she had split up with Tony, Mick allowed her to move in. Within four days, she was gone again. Life with Mick was too safe for her. Mick was upset that he couldn't give her the sense of excitement she apparently needed.

Incredibly, two weeks later, Josie was back on the doorstep of number 6. This time, she insisted, she and Tony were finished for good. Mick reacted angrily and told her to go. He would only let her stay if she was prepared to make a definite commitment to him and the kids. She apologised for her past behaviour and promised to mend her wayward ways. But before the week was out, she had another surprise for Mick. If they were going to do this properly, she said, they would have to court each other all over again. Accordingly, she moved back into her flat with the kids.

In September of 1990, Harry summoned Mick to St Helens. Mick feared the worst but Harry told him that he had decided to let the bungalow to him on a long-term basis. Showing a rarely seen streak of generosity, Harry sold Mick the furniture for £100. Mick was delighted.

Josie continued to bounce around between her flat and the bungalow like a rubber ball. One minute, she loved Tony, the next she loved Mick. It was beginning to have an effect on the kids, particularly Leo. One day, after overhearing Leo say he wished his mum and dad could get back together again, she decided to move the entire family back into the bungalow. She wasted no time in imposing her will on the place, buying new carpets and furniture to replace Harry's old stuff. To pay for them, she got a part-time job in a DIY shop. She also enrolled Leo in a new school where he was subjected to racial abuse and started bunking off.

Crisis was never far beneath the surface with the Johnsons and it bubbled over when Mick was hospitalised after being attacked in his cab. Even when he was discharged, he was still not fit enough to work, leaving them perilously short of income. Josie's attitude had always been one of spend, spend, spend. Mail-order catalogues were made for her. She ordered things like there was no tomorrow. She was determined that the family were going to have a happy Christmas and ignored Mick's pleas to send the goods back. Her best friend, Marcia Barrett, suggested that, to earn extra cash, Josie should take a part-time job with her in the notorious Fourstar Club. When Mick found out, he was livid. He didn't want Josie going anywhere near nightclubs, particularly to work. Again she ignored him and went ahead.

Two weeks before Christmas, Mick – still convalescing at home – caught a man trying to break into the children's bedroom. In the ensuing chase and struggle, the intruder was left unconscious. The Press hailed Mick as a hero but the police didn't. The burglar was prosecuting him for using 'undue force'. Mick couldn't believe it – he had only been trying to defend his home and his children. To make matters worse, they returned from a Christmas break with Josie's parents in Cardiff to face a furniture bill for £2,500, the result of Josie's free-spending. Life with Josie really was a catalogue of disasters.

The court case hung over Mick for three months. He elected for trial by jury and such was his popularity that his fellow cabbies rallied round with a collection to support him. To his immense relief, the jury found him not guilty. But a nasty shock lay just around the corner. The unscrupulous Josie had 'borrowed' the collection money to buy knocked-off children's clothes from Jimmy Corkhill for her new market stall.

The month of August 1991 was a traumatic one even by Mick's standards. It began with Gemma going missing (she was found safe and sound a few days later) and continued with a couple turning up to view the bungalow. Unbeknown to Mick, Harry had decided to sell up in order to fund a trip to Las Vegas to see Ralph and Lana. Just as Mick was taking in the implications, he received an equally unwelcome visitor – his younger brother Ellis.

Ellis had always been bad news. He was everything Mick wasn't – arrogant, devious, selfish and successful with women. When their father had walked out on the family, Mick virtually brought Ellis up. Mick had looked after him, fought his battles for him. All Ellis had ever done was cause trouble. Yet the mud always stuck to Mick, never to Ellis. He was Mr Smooth Operator, Mr Squeaky Clean. Mick resented the fact that Ellis seemed to be able to conjure up money from nowhere. He had always had it easy whereas Mick had worked hard for every penny he got. But above all, Mick resented Ellis because it was he who had introduced Josie to Tony, the man she had left Mick for. Now here he was again, in his flash car and designer clothes. Mick knew something must be up.

Within days, Mick had another house-guest. Josie invited the homeless Marcia to stay, news which put a smirk on Ellis's face. Years ago, they used to go out together. But now the man on Marcia's arm was Sinbad. Ellis, the man with a thousand chat-up lines, was very nearly lost for words. What could Marcia see in a tub of lard like Sinbad? He wasted no time in putting Sinbad down, hinting that Marcia could have a much better time if she chose to renew acquaintances with him. Although possibly tempted, Marcia stuck by Sinbad. After all, she could get a man anywhere but good window cleaners were hard to find.

The final blow for Mick came when Josie left him yet again. This time it was for good. She said she had tried to be the perfect mother and housewife but it just wasn't working out for her. She was back with Tony. Mick felt crushed.

'No wonder you always get walked all over – you just lay down and take it!'
– Marcia to Sinbad

Whereas some of the residents of the Close liked to let their fists do the talking, Ellis preferred to wound with sarcasm. Sinbad was an easy – and ample – target. Whatever he did or said, Ellis was on hand to deliver a cruel riposte. Graham Taylor got off lightly compared to Sinbad. Endeavouring to play for sympathy by acting hurt, Sinbad then got it in the neck from Marcia. She told him categorically that she was not interested in Ellis but she would like Sinbad to try and fight for her. He finally got the message and took great delight in countering one verbal assault by emptying a bucket of window-cleaning water over Ellis's head.

Sinbad had been raised in a children's home, his mother having abandoned him as a child. Now, at Marcia's suggestion, he set out to trace her. He and Marcia were told that his mother was dead but that a sister was still alive. They tracked down a Ruth Sweeney to Runcorn. She was very evasive – and with good reason. For she wasn't his sister at all. She was his long-lost mother. Elated, Sinbad (or to give him his real name, Thomas) proposed to Marcia via a message on the electronic scoreboard at Goodison Park. When she read: 'Marcia, will you please marry me? Love Sinbad', she had little option but to accept. However, their relationship foundered after she belatedly told him she couldn't have children and then she started interfering with Mick and Josie's life.

Meanwhile, Barbara and John Harrison had been on the brink of buying the

Mick Johnson Tackles a Burglar

In the run-up to Christmas 1990, so many problems piled up on Mick Johnson's doorstep that it was a wonder he could get out of the front door. After being attacked in his taxi cab, he was at home convalescing when he caught a burglar trying to break into the bungalow via the children's bedroom. Mick gave chase and in the struggle which followed, the intruder was left unconscious. Frank Rogers arrived on the scene and diagnosed that the man might be dead.

Fortunately, Frank was a better lorry-driver than doctor and the burglar recovered to press charges against Mick for using 'undue force'. Mick's faith in the law was shattered and only partially repaired when the jury eventually found him not guilty.

Leo and Gemma's room

Mick's room

1
Mick caught the burglar breaking in through Leo and Gemma's bedroom window. His instinct was to protect his family and property.

2
Mick had to endure an agonising three-month wait before the case went to court.

no. 6

bungalow before they withdrew their offer and bought number 9 instead. Mick breathed a sigh of relief. In a brotherly gesture, Ellis offered to give him the money for a deposit on a mortgage and Mick set about becoming a home-owner. There was a blip when Josie's interfering parents, the Christies, suddenly turned up from Cardiff. They were alarmed to find that Sinbad was looking after Leo and Gemma. Ellis became increasingly suspicious of the Christies' motives and, sure enough, the moment Mick's back was turned, they took the kids back to Cardiff. Borrowing Ellis's car, Mick went down to Wales and retrieved them. In his absence, Ellis disobeyed his instructions and drove the cab without a licence. Inevitably, Mick's boss found out and Mick was sacked from the cabs. As with so many things that had happened to him over the years, it was all Ellis's fault. Mick's answer was to throw him out.

When fire destroyed Manor Park Primary in the spring of 1992, Mick was outraged to hear that the school was not being rebuilt. He collected a petition and presented it to the Chairman of the Education Committee. A meeting was held at which the education department's representative, Marianne Dwyer, extolled the virtues of re-location. At the end of the meeting, she took Mick to one side and revealed that a decision to close Manor Park Primary had been made a year ago – well before the fire. Mick

responded by urging other parents to keep their children off school. Number 6 became a crèche.

The campaign fizzled out and Ellis tried to make amends for getting Mick the sack by suggesting they make a go of the pizza parlour on Brookside Parade. Ellis talked him into it but the financial burden forced Mick to consider selling the bungalow and buying the flat over the shop. Racist petrol station owner George Webb targeted the pizza parlour from the moment Mick and Ellis took it over and later phoned the Immigration Department to report illegal immigrants at 6 Brookside Close. Webb's terror campaign escalated when he set about hurling a petrol bomb into the bungalow, only to be thwarted by Ron Dixon.

Pizza king Ellis's dream topping belonged to Marianne Dwyer. They became engaged. Mick congratulated them but secretly regretted that Marianne wasn't his. Once again, Ellis had got the girl. In fact, Marianne, too, was unsure as to whether she had chosen the right brother, especially after Ellis, incensed by Webb, had tried to run him over. She was unsure as to whether she could live with such violence and found herself increasingly attracted to Mick.

Come the start of 1993, Marcia got back together with Sinbad. They planned a double Valentine's Day Wedding, alongside Marianne and Ellis. The thought of tying the knot next to Sinbad did not exactly appeal to Ellis. At the joint stag night, Mick blurted out to Sinbad that he loved Marianne. Sinbad promptly told Marcia who redoubled her efforts to get Mick reunited with Josie – there as Marcia's guest. The next day,

Sinbad accused Marcia of forcing Mick and Josie back together. Marcia dismissed Mick's declaration of love as drunken nonsense but Sinbad felt he owed it to Marianne to tell her. Besides, he'd much rather see Mick happy than Ellis. When Marcia learned that Sinbad had told Marianne, she blew her top. The wedding was off.

Josie was desperate to move back with Mick, saying she had changed. She was sure she had got her claws into him again until Marianne rushed out

Ellis Johnson courts Marianne Dwyer, but is replaced in her affections by his brother, Mick.

of the wedding ceremony, leaving Ellis stranded at the altar. Ellis had lost a bride and Josie had lost her man. It couldn't have happened to two nicer people.

After making a last-ditch attempt to snatch her kids, Josie was thrown out of number 6. Mick filed for divorce and finally got his act together with Marianne. Ellis caught them in a passionate kiss and took the hint.

Mick's money difficulties brought a threat from the building society to repossess the bungalow. Then, while Mick and Marianne were away in London for a few days, the bungalow was burgled. Mick was sick – he wasn't insured. Jimmy Corkhill confessed to carrying out the robbery – ironically he had only done it, at Ellis's suggestion, to help Mick out of his financial predicament by pulling an insurance scam. An angry Mick told the building society that they could have the bungalow. He was moving into the flat above the pizza parlour.

> 'The way feelings are running round here at the moment, your friends at number 5 are likely to be coming face to face with a lynch mob.'
> – David Crosbie, warning Barry about the religious cult

Number 6 remained empty for a month. Then in May 1993, David and Jean Crosbie, Patricia Farnham's parents, moved in. They had been staying with the Farnhams since January and, after receiving a cheque for the sale of their apartment in Spain, decided to settle in Liverpool. Fussy and pompous, David has always been something of a ladies' man. He had cheated on Jean in the past – having had an 18-month affair with Sandra, their nanny, some 20 years previously – but was hypocritical enough to condemn Max for his one-night stand with ex-wife Susannah. Jean just had to grin and bear it.

While Jean helped DD Dixon at the florist's on Brookside Parade, David struggled to fight off the attentions of Julia Brogan who adopted him as her dancing partner. She had visions of them being the next Fred and Ginger. In truth, they danced more like Fred and Wilma.

When Max and Patricia Farnham remarried in October 1993, among the guests were David's brother, Clive Crosbie, MP, with his wife Penny. They lived in Banbury. Three weeks later, Clive committed suicide, precipitating lurid tabloid headlines about the MP and a call-girl. Later he was found to have fathered a love child. Not surprisingly,

all of this came as rather a shock to Penny who sought refuge from the prying eyes of the Press, first in the Crosbies' bungalow and then next door with Max and Patricia. It didn't take journalists long to discover Penny's hiding place and, for the next few months, she was unable to set foot out of the door for fear of providing a photo opportunity.

David Crosbie established the bungalow as the headquarters of the Brookside Residents' Association (or BRA for short), arranging meetings to put pressure on first the Bankes and then Simon Howe's religious cult. In June 1994, the Crosbies celebrated their Ruby Wedding which Jean marked by confessing that she once had a relationship with another woman. David, who had already pilloried Beth Jordache and her girlfriend Chris, was suitably horrified.

Over the next couple of months, David and Jean lived separate lives. They had separate beds – David moved into Ralph's old room – and even separate meal-times. In Jean's absence David left a joint of lamb in the oven to attend Carl Banks' 21st birthday party. The only guests for dinner that day were the Fire Brigade. David went out a lot. Jean was convinced he was having another affair but in truth he was attending an over-55's afternoon social club. They were finally reconciled by the birth of Patricia's baby but when it came to resuming residency of the marital bed, David's sex drive went absent without leave. Maybe it was the ghost of Harry Cross frowning over his every move.

Following the difficult birth of Patricia's baby, the bungalow became second home to the Farnhams' eldest, Thomas, as David and Jean, the proud grandparents, did everything they could to help Max and Patricia and the new baby. But Jean was busy with other activities. She was an invaluable member of the All Ladies Brookside Darts Team and she started running her own over-55's club at La Luz. David's little problem would just have to wait . . .

Jean Crosbie stirs up a hornet's nest at number 6 by showing David letters from her lesbian friend.

number 7

The majority of people like to move into a house with a minimum of fuss. Not Harry Cross. When he took the keys to 7 Brookside Close in the autumn of 1983, it was a day neither the other residents nor the removal men would forget in a hurry. It began with Edna insulting the men, as a result of which they dumped her things on the pavement and drove off. Then Harry noticed that his boxing medals were missing. Jumping to conclusions was to become a speciality of Harry's and he showed early tendencies in that direction by immediately accusing Damon Grant and his pal Gizzmo of stealing them. In fact, the culprit was Gordon Collins's friend, Mark Gossage. When Mark returned the medals, he and Damon got into a brawl on the Crosses' front lawn, egged on by Harry himself, eager to display his knowledge of the Queensberry Rules.

Barely had the dust settled than Marie Jackson's unruly sons Gary and Little George started relocating Harry's beloved garden gnomes. Edna and Marie came back from the shops to see that the gnomes had 'walked' into Heather's garden. They began to spring up everywhere, even in trees. Marie automatically blamed Damon and when the finger was pointed at her own offspring, she further antagonised Harry by calling his gnomes 'dwarfs'. As Harry was to discover to his cost, the Jacksons weren't the last boys to find his gnomes irresistible.

But the big shock for Harry was discovering that his son Kevin, a teacher at a school in Maghull, was living with a married woman, Sally Haynes, and her daughter Jessica. Harry did not approve of such goings-on and when Jessica came to visit one day, he stubbornly refused to let her in and shut the door in her face. Edna was upset at Harry's behaviour but she knew full well that nothing she said would ever make him change his mind. She had more chance of getting Arthur Scargill to vote Tory.

Harry's heart condition encouraged him to buy the bungalow and to let out number 7 to tenants. Having been tricked into accepting hospital porter Pat Hancock as the third lodger, along with young nurses Kate Moses and Sandra Maghie, Harry proceeded to spy on them at every opportunity. He used his key to let himself in whether they were there or not, marching through the house like an army of occupation. He read their letters, opened their cupboards, ate their biscuits. It was his right, he said, as a landlord. It was his house. Pat insisted that he hand over the key and when Harry refused, the nurses decided to have the locks changed.

The ill fated Kate Moses.

The Farnhams re-marry, to the apparent delight of son Thomas.

Sandra, who was Scottish and separated, and Kate, who was West Indian and single, were intelligent, hard-working girls. Sandra was perhaps the more forceful and street-wise of the two, Kate being rather reserved, at least to outsiders. Although their circumstances were different (Sandra had an unhappy marriage behind her whereas Kate came from a close-knit family), the girls got on well together. The fly in the ointment was usually Pat. He was something of a chancer whose mode of transport, a battered old ambulance, soon ruffled Paul Collins's feathers. Among his other curious possessions was a human skeleton which he liked to dress up. A startled Harry stumbled across it on one of his spying missions. Pat was an outwardly likeable but occasionally hot-headed Cockney with a propensity for wearing a vest in order to flash his bulging biceps at passing females. He was always on the lookout for ways of making a fast buck to support his meagre hospital income. With that goal, he had no shortage of accomplices on Brookside Close.

On one occasion, Kate was disturbed to discover a 'pre-op' patient eating a Chinese takeaway. The patient was not supposed to be eating anything at all. Her investigations revealed that Pat had been running a scam with another porter, Dougie, whereby they sold food to patients. The conscientious Kate threatened to report the pair of them.

Another of Pat's grandiose schemes was to set up a kissogram service. He bought some costumes from a theatrical shop and persuaded Damon to be a gorilla at a children's party. He also hired a 'naughty nurse', much to the disgust of Sandra and Kate who labelled him sexist. Leaving a booking one night, he realised his ambulance had been stolen. Sandra usually relied on him for a lift home if she was on the late shift but when he failed to show, she accepted one from radiographer Jimmy Powell instead. On the way, Powell stopped the car and made a grab for her. She hit out and managed to escape. When Pat arrived at the hospital in a taxi, Sandra accused him of encouraging men to attack women.

The next day, Pat sought retribution and lashed out at Powell, breaking some expensive equipment in the process. Pat was suspended from duty before being formally sacked.

Sandra had a lot of problems with men. Her husband Ian had been demanding a divorce for some months and one day turned up on her doorstep, having driven down from Glasgow. She refused to consider a divorce, whereupon he hit her. Her knight in shining armour, Pat, came

down and threw him out. Ian retaliated by announcing that he would sue for divorce, citing Pat as co-respondent. A couple of weeks later, Sandra received another visit – this time from her husband's Asian girl-friend, Hina Narayan, who explained that unless she could marry soon, she would be forced to leave Britain. Sandra considered that she was being subjected to emotional blackmail. Later, Sandra heard that Hina had managed to obtain a work permit after all, but still wanted to marry Ian.

Harry's concern about shenanigans at number 7 seemed ill-founded. The general air was one of depression rather than merriment. For with Pat out of work, the trio were struggling to pay the rent. To make matters worse, whoever stole Pat's ambulance had written it off.

'I want me mum. She's the only one who can help me. I want me mum! I want me mum! I want me mum!'
– John Clarke at the height
of the siege

For a day out in July 1985, they decided to visit the Alder Hey Hospital Fête where they met a middle-aged man by the name of John Clarke. He was a weird character who recognised Kate as one of the nurses on duty when his mother had died at the hospital. Clarke was obsessed by his mother. He seemed to be blaming Kate and the other nurses for her death. Kate lost her temper, saying that it was nobody's fault. His mother had simply been too ill to be saved. Clarke's aggression remained controlled but Pat sensed that it might explode at any minute and managed to steer the girls away.

If they thought they were free of Clarke, they were sorely mistaken. He found out their address and decided to pay them a visit. Sandra was in the house alone when he arrived. She was reluctant to let him in but he insisted that he just wanted to apologise for his behaviour the other day. He appeared calm and rational. She was happy to accept his apology and say goodbye but then he suggested a cup of tea. It dawned on her that he was not going to leave. His mood became more menacing. The others returned home. When Pat tried to throw him out, Clarke pulled a gun.

The three were prisoners. The tense atmosphere was interrupted by a knock on the front door. It was Harry, informing his tenants that he was imposing a rent increase. Pat knew that with Clarke pointing a gun at the girls, the best thing was to get rid of Harry as quickly as possible. So he agreed unreservedly to the increase. Harry trotted off, scarcely able to believe how easy it had all been while Pat closed the door on the outside world, steeling himself to face the ordeal ahead.

Trussed up and with Clarke growing more manic by the minute, the nurses spent a terrifying night. The slightest thing could push him over the edge. Pat nearly did just that when he tried to play the hero. It was not a role to which Pat was suited. In spite of the fact that the curtains remained drawn during the day, none of the neighbours suspected anything. Except Annabelle Collins, that is. At first, Paul dismissed her fears but after a few days, she finally persuaded him to call in the police who wasted no time in evacuating the Close. The residents were despatched to a nearby boarding house where they watched the siege on television.

Pat was the first to crack. At one point, Kate had actually seemed to be getting through to Clarke but Pat panicked and wrecked everything. Kate persisted with her efforts to bring everything to a peaceful conclusion. As Pat crumbled, Kate grew in stature. Eventually, she talked Clarke into releasing Pat and Sandra. Perhaps the end was in sight. But then while the police were attempting to ascertain whether the gun was real, Clarke's mood suddenly changed. He said he was going to shoot himself. Kate, compassionate to the last, tried to stop him. Three gun shots rang out across the Close. Cautiously, the police entered the house. Upstairs, in Kate's bedroom, they found her and Clarke dead.

Brookside Close was front page news. The Press were out in force. The air was heavy with expense forms. Pat and Sandra sought refuge with Terry at number 10 until the heat died down. Both were still in a state of shock. They felt they could have done more – Pat in particular blamed himself for Kate's death. So did Kate's sister, Debbie. At Kate's funeral, Debbie left him with the impression that he should have been the one to take control of the situation. They were calling him a coward and the worse thing was, he had to agree. In frustration, he lashed out at a prying journalist.

Sandra and Pat began to find comfort in each other's arms. Sandra went to stay with her mother in Glasgow but started to miss Pat. The feeling was mutual and, out of the blue, Pat turned up in Glasgow. Sandra arranged for Pat to stay with her friend, Fiona, but got annoyed when Fiona made a play for him. Things were getting serious between Sandra and Pat. They had been brought together in adversity and now, the first time they found themselves alone, they ended up in bed.

The arrangement continued when they returned to Liverpool. They invited Terry to move in with them but nobody slept in Kate's room. It was left untouched, a shrine to her courage.

Seeking to put the tragedy behind him, Pat embarked on a van-hire business with Terry, borrowing £2,000 from the bank. They landed a contract ferrying around fruit machines for Mike Henty of Hentytainments but trouble was not far away. They started receiving bogus jobs, sending them to exotic locations such as Wrexham, and their van was vandalised. Then they were paid a visit by the glamorous Vicki Cleary from the van firm which used to have the Henty contract. She accused Pat and Terry of behaving unfairly and stealing her business. It transpired that the Clearys were behind the aggravation.

Vicki tried to resolve the van war but Pat gave her short shrift. To Pat's disgust, Terry was far more conciliatory and took Vicki for a drink. Pat enlisted the help of Barry Grant and while Terry was doing his Henry Kissinger routine, Pat and Barry were planning to bring the matter to a more violent conclusion. Catching Joe and Eddy Cleary sabotaging the van outside a café, Pat and Barry beat them up. At Vicki's instigation, her brothers met Terry to do a deal but, at the same time, back at the Clearys' yard, Barry was smashing up a van. Sadly for him, it was the wrong van – it didn't belong to the Clearys. And neither Pat nor Terry were prepared to cough up the money to pay for the damage.

Harry still kept a watch on comings and goings but one who slipped through his net was Barry's ex-girlfriend Jane, a heroin addict. She stayed at number 7 for a while and, desperate for money, offered her body to Terry for £20. He decided she was over-priced. He'd wait for the sales. Soon Pat and Sandra opted to get rid of Jane but discovered that she had beaten them to it and had taken some of their valuables with her. Few tears were shed over her departure.

Terry's presence in the house slowly created a rift between Pat and Sandra. It was nothing that Terry had done, simply that when he was around, Pat tended to behave differently. It was a case of 'lads together' with the result that Sandra was either taken for granted or ignored completely. Also, she and Pat were hardly ever able to be on their own. All in all, Sandra was becoming highly disillusioned with the arrangement. And she was not the sort of girl to keep her feelings to herself. She and Pat began to have some fearful barneys.

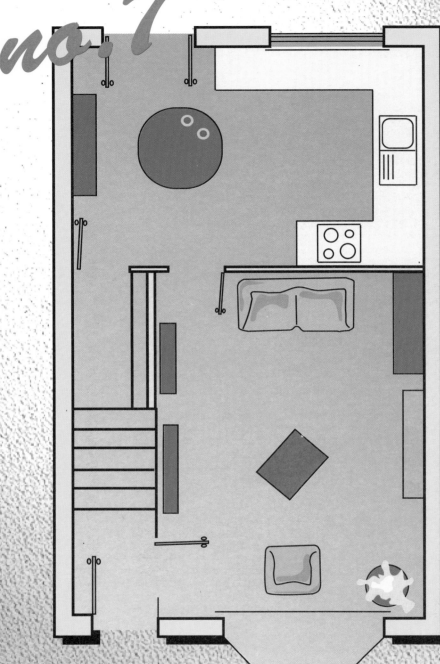

1

When Clarke first arrived, Sandra was alone in the house. There was no sign of a gun. He insisted on making a cup of tea and it dawned on her that he was not going to leave in a hurry.

The Siege

On a summer's day in 1985, a knock on the door of number 7 was to herald a terrifying and ultimately tragic ordeal for Pat Hancock, Sandra Maghie and Kate Moses. The caller was John Clarke, a middle-aged man still disturbed by the recent death of his mother at the hospital where the three worked. In fact, he blamed them for her death.

The trio were held at gunpoint by Clarke and, as neighbours became concerned about the lack of activity at the house, the police were called in and the Close was evacuated. Kate tried to strike a rapport with Clarke which led to Pat and Sandra being released. With the police thinking about moving in, gun shots rang out. Clarke had shot Kate and then himself. The siege of Brookside Close had left two dead and two more mentally scarred for years to come.

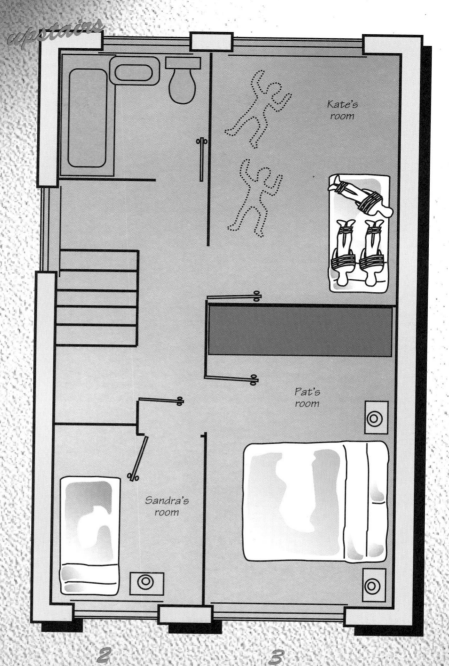

upstairs

Kate's
room

Pat's
room

Sandra's
room

2
The three were
tied up in Kate's
bedroom.

3
Clarke and Kate died
from gun shot wounds
in Kate's bedroom,
which was to become a
shrine to her courage.

It came as little surprise therefore when she took an interest in work colleague Dr Tony Hurrell. Quietly spoken, courteous and intelligent, he was a cut above Pat. But then sometimes so was Godzilla. The relationship with Tony Hurrell started innocently enough. The pair discovered that an eminent surgeon at the hospital, Mr Cribbs-Baker, had been carrying out unnecessary operations in the private wards for his own financial gain. They decided they could not turn a blind eye to this gross malpractice and set about collating sufficient evidence. They would need plenty to topple somebody of the status of Cribbs-Baker but Sandra was not one to shirk a challenge. They met regularly at number 7, poring over documents to the exclusion of Pat. He could see them becoming closer. Suddenly the case was the only thing in the world that seemed to matter to Sandra.

Pat's jealousy erupted into violent rages. He started hitting Sandra. It was after one such row, which left him with scratch marks on his face, that he was questioned by police investigating the rape of Sheila Grant. Sandra felt that he could have been capable of it – and that frightened her. Ian had been the same – he used to knock her about. Pat promised that it would never happen again, but it was too late. She was not going to live with another wife-beater.

On the rebound, Pat took up with an older woman, Andrea Parkin, wife of the chairman of the local amateur football club for whom he played. He thought nothing of climbing into bed with Andrea even though Sandra was in the house. Petulantly, he asked Sandra to move out, saying he felt inhibited by her presence. She refused.

The case against Cribbs-Baker had collapsed. Tony Hurrell had been warned off pursuing his quest for justice and had decided to quit Liverpool. He came round to say goodbye to Sandra and they finished up in bed. Despite what Pat had thought, it was the first time she and Tony had slept together. Sandra made up her mind to leave with Tony and, in September 1986, just over a year after the siege, they departed for Scotland.

Andrea soon dumped Pat but it was more than his ego which risked being bruised when he and Terry received a call from Tommy McArdle, the camel-coated 'businessman' who was likely to get the hump if he didn't get his own way. McArdle had arranged for Dutton, the taxi driver who raped Sheila, to be beaten up but in return he expected a favour from Barry Grant. Since he was conveniently off on one of his disappearing acts, Barry passed the job on to Terry.

Despite Terry's natural misgivings about getting involved again in anything remotely connected with Tommy McArdle (he had already sampled hospital food courtesy of McArdle in the wake of the George Jackson trial), this task seemed straightforward enough. All he and Pat had to do was accompany Tommy's old mum to Barbados. It turned out that Mrs M, far from being a harmless old dear, was acting as a courier for Tommy. She collected an envelope in Barbados, hid it in a suitcase and got Terry to carry it home through customs. Terry had suspected her senility was just an act but was given no support by Pat who had eyes only for dusky tourist guide Avril. Adhering to his usual 'act now, think later' philosophy, Pat contemplated staying in Barbados just so that he could be with Avril. She was more practical.

Back in Liverpool, Harry Cross was waiting for his rent. The boys were in arrears and, with Sandra gone, they decided to advertise for a new tenant. Pat thought he'd struck lucky – not with a woman for once – when he recruited Mike and Mick, two kiln builders who worked on opposite shifts. Consequently, they only needed one bed, and Pat and Terry collected one and a half times the rent. It should have been an arrangement made in heaven but Mick, who kept a noisy pet macaw, was a slob with irritating habits while Mike's chat-up

Terry Sullivan – forever unlucky in love.

techniques threatened to encroach upon Pat's domain. Pat and Terry did their best to keep the existence of Mick, who worked nights, a secret from Harry so that they could keep the extra cash but when Terry's girlfriend Vicki, fed up with the new lodgers, issued an ultimatum, the kiln builders were on their way out.

Pat had always been keen on the music scene – he could remember when George was still a Boy and Johnny was still Rotten. He fancied himself as a bit of a singer and, after a chance meeting in the pub, took on the role of roadie to Fran and her all-girl group. Before long, he had blackmailed the other girls, Ellie and Trish, into letting him be their backing singer. It was either that or they lost the van. They soon regretted allowing him to join as he proceeded to upstage them at every possible opportunity. While Pat was trying to make sweet music with Fran, Terry and Vicki were splitting up. Vicki had been becoming increasingly frustrated with Pat. In the end, she issued another of her celebrated ultimatums, telling Terry that the only way she would move in with him was if he got rid of Pat both as a co-tenant and as a business partner. Terry, who never put off a decision until tomorrow if he could put it off until the following month, dithered some more and Vicki walked out of his life.

Pat wasn't around for much longer either. Having discovered they were swindling him over Mike and Mick, Harry wanted to buy out Pat and Terry. Pat, who by now was dreaming of becoming the next George Michael, was thinking about moving on anyway and so whilst he rejected Harry's initial offer of £100, he hinted that if Harry were to dip his hand a little deeper into his pocket, he would be sorely tempted. Within a month, Harry came up with £500. Pat nearly bit his hand off. In September 1987, he left the Close but not before he had wrecked his chances with Fran by trying to double-cross the other two girls. During his time on the Close, Pat trod on more toes than Harry Cross at a tea dance. He would never learn.

Harry had planned to sell number 7 to Alison, Terry's latest girlfriend, but when she announced that she was going back to her husband, he was left high and dry. He responded by giving Terry notice to quit. Being Terry, he didn't stray far – only to number 9 where Jonathan Gordon-Davies took him in.

Forced to seek new tenants, Harry reckoned that Frank and Chrissy Rogers would come up to scratch. As a friendly gesture, he baked a cake to mark their arrival but the goodwill evaporated the moment he saw them turn up in an articulated lorry. Come back, Pat and Terry, all is forgiven!

Geoff Rogers was a particular thorn in Harry's side. After being caught abseiling down the side of the house, he and his mate

One of his many business exploits – Terry runs a taxi cab with neigbour, Mick Johnson.

Bumper accidentally set fire to the post box. On another occasion, Harry caught him hanging his garden gnomes from a tree. Chrissy soon marched into battle on her kids' behalf, rowing with the school over daughter Sammy's new, non-regulation school coat and about Geoff's lack of progress.

Frank, meanwhile, was pushing for the desk job he had been promised, only for his case to be severely damaged when his lorry was stolen. He was charged with serious misconduct and severely reprimanded but he held on to his job. Not much chance of promotion though. Chrissy was so disgusted by the spineless union rep who defended him that she implored Frank to stand for the union. It was a move she would live to regret.

When his romantic tea with Betty Parkinson was interrupted by Frank complaining about the hot water system, Harry decided he'd had enough of the pressures of being a landlord. It was definitely time to sell. Working at the estate agents, Chrissy was more than a little surprised to find her home suddenly appearing on the market. She urged Frank to act swiftly and put in an offer for number 7. For once in their lives, they were not flat broke. Sammy had just started work at a local supermarket

Harry Cross thought Frank Rogers and his family would be the perfect tenants – he was soon to be proved wrong.

and money was coming in steadily if not spectacularly. But Harry had seen enough of the Rogers family to last him a lifetime. The last straw had been when Geoff had stolen Ralph's model of the Close. So, rejecting their offer out of hand, Harry instead issued them with a notice to quit.

Harry Cross was a wily old fox but, as he was to find to his cost, Chrissy Rogers could be devious too. So after he had refused her offer above the asking price, she made another offer anonymously, this time slightly below the asking price. Harry accepted it gratefully. He thought he had finally got shot of them. Chrissy and Frank could hardly contain themselves. Putting one over on Harry deserved a lap of honour round the Close but Frank had a more subtle plan. On the day of the move, he got the family and neighbours dressed up as Arabs. Harry couldn't understand why Chrissy was taking it all so calmly until he realised the true identity of the men from the Middle East. Discovering he had been duped, Harry went home and sulked.

Within six months, 7 Brookside Close did have an Eastern flavour when Michael, Caroline and Jessica Choi took up residence in May 1989, the Rogers family having bought number 5. Thinking they were Japanese, Harry immediately dispatched Ralph to the timber merchants to erect a six-foot high fence. After all, he didn't want Pearl Harbor being re-enacted in his garden pond. Before Ralph could go, however, Harry discovered that not only were the Chois Chinese, but also that Michael was a doctor. The old hypochondriac warmed to them considerably – and ordered the fence to be reduced to a more modest 18 inches.

Michael and Caroline were brother and sister. He was a widower, his wife Meilin having been killed in a road accident six months previously. Due to his busy work schedule, he relied on Caroline to look after his five-year-old daughter Jessica. But Caroline wanted a life of her own – the chance to further her jewellery-making business – she was tired of playing the role of surrogate mother. What she wanted was some independence. Against this background of tension, it was not altogether surprising that their arrival on the Close was fraught with difficulties. Jessica went off unannounced to play with Katie Rogers, leaving Michael frantic about her whereabouts. When Jessica eventually turned up, Caroline blamed Chrissy – hardly the best of starts for the new neighbours. Later, Michael and Caroline argued and, after a few home truths, Caroline stormed out of the Close.

She was soon back but the tension remained. She decided to take the bull by the horns and discussed Jessica's future with Michael's parents-in-law in Hong Kong. They wanted the child with them but Michael was adamant that her place was with him. It seemed that Caroline's feelings were irrelevant. Soon after they had moved in, Jessica was off school sick and Caroline was forced to take the girl with her on her business rounds. Caroline lost her temper after the child began mithering. The situation provoked another row with Michael who demanded to know what Caroline's priorities were – work or Jessica. Matters came to a head when Caroline asked Chrissy Rogers, with whom she was now friends, to look after Jess while she went out to work. Chrissy agreed, but when Caroline failed to return on time, she was forced to leave Jess with Michael, otherwise she herself would have been late for work. An angry Michael had no choice but to take Jess to the surgery with him. It was most inconvenient for him.

Out shopping one day, Michael saw an old lady collapse. He and a young woman, Alison, tried to resuscitate her but the old lady died in hospital. Michael set out to find the mysterious Alison in order to tell her what had happened. Her name was Alison Gregory and it was quickly apparent that she and Michael were attracted to each other. Alison, too, was a single parent, with an eight-year-old daughter, Hattie.

Meanwhile, Caroline had a less likely suitor – Sinbad. His heart melted when she allowed him to do a few odd jobs for her and when he mucked them up, he apologised in the only way he knew. Flowers? Chocolates? No, he cleaned her windows free of charge. What more could a girl want? He even acted as emergency entertainment at Jessica's sixth birthday party after the magician he had booked failed to turn up.

If Caroline Choi was the

sweet, Michael's father Stephen was definitely the sour. A restauranteur, he was a strict traditionalist who disapproved of just about everything Michael did, particularly his blossoming relationship with an English girl. Instead he tried to push Michael into the arms of Amy Ying, the daughter of an old family friend. Although wary of his father, Michael had a mind of his own. He wanted to be with Alison, despite the fact that she had been offered a scientific research post in America. The solution seemed to be for Michael to go too, a proposition which infuriated Stephen who began using Jessica as an innocent pawn in his plot to wreck the romance. Above all, Stephen could not permit Jessica to be taken to such a decadent land as the United States.

In October 1989, Caroline returned from a trip to Hong Kong to find that Alison and Hattie had moved in with Michael. Caroline too expressed her reservations, warning Alison that she could be making a big mistake by marrying into a different culture.

The family disputes had been having an adverse effect on Caroline's business. She had just not been able to devote sufficient time to it. In a move indicative of his changing stance, Michael offered to find a childminder for Jess – something which had previously been out of the question. Another possible boost to Caroline's career was the arrival of an ex-boyfriend, James Markham. No sooner had he come back into her life than he proposed marriage. Sinbad was most put out, realising that a chamois leather, a bucket and a ladder could hardly compete with expensive clothes, a healthy bank account and a flash car.

In fact, far from being healthy, James's bank account was on a life-support machine.

In 1990, Max and Patricia Farnham moved into 7 Brookside Close.

And the manager was poised to switch it off. He kept this minor detail carefully hidden from Caroline as he wormed his way into the position of her business manager. Sinbad didn't trust him – a feeling which Caroline attributed to the green-eyed monster, even when she learned of a stack of video nasties in the boot of James's car. Then she discovered that her jewellery was being sold with fake stones. Positive that her outworkers couldn't be responsible, she asked James to investigate. He found a sacrificial lamb but was merely delaying the inevitable. Caroline did some checking of her own and found that James was behind the fraud, needing to pay off £5,000 in gambling debts. Desperate for the cash, he stole Caroline's car but, with his shady business associates in hot pursuit of him and their money, he was killed in a car crash in Aberdeen. The police treated it as suspected murder.

In April 1990, Caroline Choi left the Close and Michael put the house up for sale in preparation for his departure to America with Alison. He and his father had been reunited. Michael refused to give Caroline's new address to Sinbad and so, in Michael's absence, he put off a couple of prospective house buyers with tales of subsidence and rot. Gatecrashing Michael's farewell party in order to collect his window money, Sinbad craftily pocketed the back door key. Stephen Choi then displayed a worrying lack of judgement by installing Sinbad as official caretaker. His first deed was to allow Jimmy Corkhill the run of the place.

Naturally it was in Sinbad's interests to delay the sale of the house for as long as possible. That way, he kept a roof over his head. So likely buyers were greeted with a catalogue of house ills – everything from rising damp to death watch beetle. Chrissy Rogers was becoming increasingly suspicious as to why none of her clients seemed interested and, after an attempted barbecue had left the place in a state, Stephen Choi evicted Sinbad and Jimmy.

The new owners, Max and Patricia Farnham, moved in with their son Thomas and live-in nanny, Margaret Clemence, on 12 September 1990. Quantity surveyor and prominent member of the Round Table, Max was beset with money problems from day one – so much so that he attempted to get the asking price reduced by a few thousand pounds. Women were Max's downfall – there were too many of them in his life and they all cost money. He had met his first wife, Susannah, while they were both sixth formers studying for their 'A' Levels. They married soon after and in no time at all Susannah was pregnant. They moved out of her flat, into their first house but barely had they unpacked than Susannah fell pregnant again. Perhaps sensing the chance of a place in the *Guinness Book of Records*, Max began casting his rod further afield and embarked on an affair with the lovely Patricia.

Continuing to sow more seeds than Percy Thrower in his heyday, Max proceeded to make Patricia pregnant with equal haste. A bitter divorce with Susannah ensued, she being determined to have her pound of flesh. Max's maintenance payments were crippling but even so, he and Patricia realised that they needed a house with a garden in which Thomas could play. Hence the move to Brookside Close.

Max loved Patricia dearly but in moments of reflection, couldn't help feeling guilty about the way in which Susannah had given up on her studies just for him, and how he had repaid that faith and commitment by abandoning her, leaving her with two children and no career.

Unlike Susannah, Patricia did have a career, working for an advertising agency. Outwardly, she was supremely confident, to the point of aloofness with some of the less desirable neighbours, but inside she was terribly insecure. She dreaded losing Max to another woman. She had stolen him from Susannah and the thought was always in the back of her mind that the same thing might happen again, this time to her. She even feared that he might go back to Susannah because, although he constantly complained about the payments he had to make to his ex-wife, there was clearly still a chemistry between them. Indeed Patricia later admitted that she only really got pregnant as a guarantee that Max would not go back to his family. She saw the baby as her one way of keeping him. Maybe she was over-optimistic. After all, he had already walked out on two children. But Max still loved Matthew and Emily and liked to see them as often as possible. This, of course, meant going through Susannah – and any contact between Max and Susannah had Patricia scurrying for the valium.

The day of the move was interrupted by Patricia being summoned in to work 'for an hour'. Without her around to look after him, Max got in a right state with the removal men, the result being that all of the furniture ended up in the wrong rooms. Patricia arrived home to find the house in chaos but Max proudly showing off his newly-erected garden shed. He was like a child with a new toy. And she loved him for it.

While Max was playing with another toy – a burglar alarm he had installed – Patricia

Two knights of the Round Table, Jimmy Corkhill and Sinbad, kidnap Max's sleigh for a spot of fund-raising of their own.

was already having a few misgivings about the house. Although it was three-bedroomed, it somehow seemed smaller than she had imagined. But that was nothing compared to the misgivings she had when their new next-door neighbours moved in. She and Max were enjoying an intimate evening alone when they were rudely interrupted by a loud bang – the backfiring of the Dixons' van. The Moby had arrived in town.

Poor Max. He was a grade one snob who had assumed the mantle from Paul Collins as if he was to the manner born. He had puffed himself up in front of the neighbours, only to be deflated by a tribe who would have given 10 Rillington Place a bad name. He knew that Susannah's financial dictates would leave him on his uppers but he had no idea that he could sink this low. Through gritted teeth, he described the Dixons as being something out of 'The Beverly Hillbillies'. He christened them 'the Clampitts'. It was not a term of endearment.

Patricia was equally horrified, particularly when Ron Dixon referred to them as 'Maxie' and 'Pat'. She was not a Pat or a Trish, she was a Patricia. Margaret, the Farnhams' nanny, was more receptive and allowed Ron to park the Moby on the Farnhams' drive. For that, she got a flea in her ear from her employers. A friendly, obliging girl, Margaret nevertheless had to ensure that she was not being taken advantage of by the Farnhams. Encouraged by her friend Sammy Rogers, she went on a work-

to-rule over the issue of ironing Max's shirts. Max got hot under the collar.

Not that it needed much to send Max into a panic, especially if he thought his standing in the community was at risk. Shortly after moving in, he was appalled to find that their address was on a credit black-list, as a result of which they couldn't even buy a new dishwasher. Patricia blamed Josie Johnson and received a kick in the shin for her pains. For Josie, actions always spoke louder than words. The culprits turned out to be Jimmy and Sinbad who had been operating a catalogue scam from the house before the Farnhams moved in. Then, on his first Christmas in the Close, Max was left in charge of the Round Table charity sleigh. He was bursting with pride – that is, until it went missing from outside his house, borrowed by Jimmy and Sinbad. Forced to take his Table colleagues out to dinner rather than face the ignominy of admitting that he had lost the sleigh, Max was mightily relieved when it later magically reappeared. This time, he tethered it to a lamp-post.

Restless at work and needing extra cash to pay for the second-hand car he had just bought Patricia, Max took a job with the electricity board. The salary was £3,000 more, sufficient to give Margaret a rise and

1

While the cat's away –
Margaret and Derek
decided to make the
most of having the
house to themselves
for the evening.

Margaret and Derek

Following a couple of false starts (one interrupted by a red-faced Max), the Farnhams' nanny Margaret Clemence, finally succeeded in defrocking Father Derek O'Farrell in the summer of 1992. To celebrate this relinquishing of the priesthood, the pair jumped into Margaret's bed at number 7 and enjoyed the experience so much that they came back for more a few days later while Max and Patricia were out dining Patricia's boss, Karyn Clark.

This time they were in for a nasty shock. Derek was not used to such activity and dozed off in the afterglow. They were still asleep in each other's arms when the Farnhams returned. Peeved Patricia and mad Max were not amused to find that while their nanny had been otherwise engaged, son Thomas had been sick. It was time they found a new nanny.

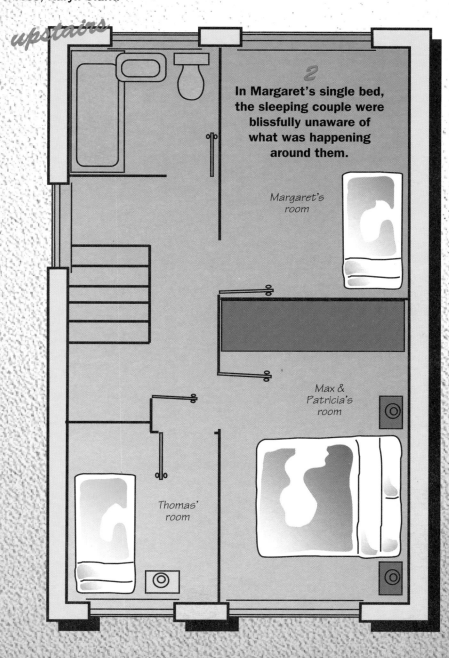

upstairs

2

In Margaret's single bed, the sleeping couple were blissfully unaware of what was happening around them.

Margaret's room

Max & Patricia's room

Thomas' room

also to cater for Susannah's increasingly expensive tastes. If Max was lucky, there might be a couple of bob left for him.

If such a thing were possible, relations with the Dixons were actually deteriorating. Young Tony Dixon delighted in pricking Max's pomposity at every available opportunity and rigged his garden shed so that it fell down when the door was opened. And as Max set off for his first day in his new job, he found himself blocked in by Mike Dixon's car. There was a threat of solicitors at dawn. Max quickly realised that the electricity board job was a ghastly mistake. Within a month, he had handed in his notice. Patricia, too, was unhappy at work. She had been working hard on a campaign for toxic waste, only to be informed by her boss, Paul Cunningham, that she had been put on impregnated mopheads instead. Cunningham made it clear that he considered a mother's place to be at home. Patricia's feelings were a mixture of fury, tinged with a degree of guilt at having to leave Thomas every day. This guilt sometimes erupted in an unwarranted attack on Margaret. The Farnhams worried that Thomas would pick up Margaret's Oldham accent and Patricia criticised her for using 'baby talk' words. Although he was still being potty-trained, in Patricia's mind he should have been thumbing through Roget's *Thesaurus* by now.

Having resigned from the electricity board, Max busied himself with fitting a new kitchen, in the course of which a council lorry arrived on the Close. The men wanted to know which rubbish Max wanted moving. He told them to take everything and they unwittingly removed some of the Dixons' prized possessions. When he found out that it was a Mr Farnham who had asked for the rubbish to be taken away, Ron Dixon created medical history by having kittens. Ron was not one to take such an act of provocation lying down and he retaliated by erecting a hideous wall between the two houses, made up of garishly-painted old doors. This was war.

Margaret Clemence fends off the unwelcome advances of Kieran, her old boyfriend from Oldham.

While the neighbourly feud raged, Max had more serious things on his mind, like finding a new job. This became of paramount importance after Patricia announced that she had been offered promotion . . . in London. Max tried to dissuade her from accepting but, annoyed by his selfish attitude, she took the post on a month's trial. She said that the way things were going, with him out of work, she could end up paying maintenance for his kids. So he swallowed his pride and rang a Round Table colleague, Geoffrey Fletcher, fishing for work. Geoffrey came up trumps but only just in time. Max had to race down to London and tell Patricia before she accepted the job on a permanent basis. Hearing his pleas and assurances, she agreed to turn it down.

> 'You know how I feel about you, don't you? I'm not just some silly little Catholic schoolgirl who fancies you just cos you're different from all the other priests. I'm me. I'm Margaret. I really feel strongly about you.'
>
> – Margaret Clemence to Derek O'Farrell

Margaret had always been keen on boys but part of the reason she had left her native Oldham was to escape from the clutches of her boyfriend Kieran who had wanted to get engaged. Kieran was also extremely physical and Margaret was unsure about that side of a relationship. In the summer of 1991, she met Father Derek O'Farrell, a handsome young priest who had come to visit his older sister, DD Dixon. They became friends. She liked his warmth and honesty and besides, she felt safe with him. He was one fella who was not going to leap on her. Together they allowed peace and harmony to return to the Close by dismantling Ron Dixon's wall, only for their friendship to create a larger, more insurmountable barrier between the two families.

For Margaret was falling in love with Derek. She started to pine when he was not around and began travelling miles to his parish in order to see him. At first, he was blissfully unaware of her true feelings – he simply saw her as a friend, someone who wanted to help the Church. In time, it dawned on him that she did have romantic inclinations. He tried to fight it, warning her that their friendship was dangerous, all the more so when Father Thornton, the parish priest, became suspicious.

But Margaret would not be denied. She was not some silly girl with a crush on the unattainable, no matter what DD Dixon thought. DD had tried to frighten Margaret off right from the start and as she saw that her words were not getting through, her attitude progressed from cool to openly hostile. A zealous Catholic herself, she was not going to stand by and watch her brother throw his life and his faith away on a young girl, and so she conducted her own Brookside Inquisition to keep Margaret and Derek apart. As Derek's resistance began to crumble, Margaret confided in Patricia who arranged clandestine meetings between the unlikely lovers.

Inevitably, DD found out and went straight to parish priest Father Thornton. Derek was posted to Grasmere in the Lake District. DD felt confident that would be the end of the matter.

In fact, it had the opposite effect. Despite antagonism from her own mother, Margaret told Derek that he had to choose between her and the church. After much soul-searching, he chose Margaret and relinquished the priesthood. To underline his decision, he and Margaret made love at the Farnhams'. Unfortunately, Patricia returned to find that Thomas had been sick. And where was her nanny? In bed with a lapsed priest!

Meanwhile Patricia was feeling increasingly threatened by Susannah who suddenly seemed to be seeing more of Max than when they had been married. Partly due to pressures of work and partly due to sheer pig-headedness, Patricia refused to accompany Max to an important Round Table function. 'All the Table wives will be there,' implored Max, but this time his pleas fell on deaf ears. Geoffrey Fletcher could not allow Max to turn up alone – it was bad for the Round Table image – and so he arranged for Susannah to resume the role of Mrs Farnham . . . for one night only. A stunned Max made him promise never to tell Patricia but eventually she found out. She decided it was time for a face-to-face with the ex-wife and laid down the ground rules as to when Susannah could see Max. Susannah countered by telling Patricia that she could win Max back any time she wanted. She might not have had his ring any more but she had still got Max wrapped around her finger.

Patricia's insecurity was heightened when she had to stay overnight in London following a presentation. Phoning home to wish Max sweet dreams, she was stunned to hear Susannah pick up the receiver. Patricia slammed the phone down and sobbed her heart out in her hotel room. To make matters worse, she had discovered a lump on her breast.

bedroom followed by an equally dishev-
elled, worried-looking Peter. Later she
accused him of rape. The repercussions
were felt all around the Close, not least at
number 7 where the Farnhams' duvet was
taken away for evidence. As a gesture of
support, Patricia asked Diana to move in
with them pending the trial, a move
which not go down well with Anna
who was firmly on Peter's side over the
rape case. When Anna asked Patricia for
a day off to attend court, Patricia told
her that she would have to choose between
going to court and losing her job. Shortly
afterwards, Patricia found the excuse
she had been looking for all along and
sacked Anna.

Margaret and Derek had become
engaged and while she found another post
nannying, he took a voluntary job with
Catholic Aid for Overseas Development. A
trip to Romania beckoned. DD even
coughed up Margaret's airfare but in the
end, Margaret couldn't bear to leave. Derek
went to Romania alone. Following the ill-
fated relationship with Beth Jordache,
during which they went to bed at the
Farnhams', Margaret finally decided to join
Derek overseas in Bosnia.

In August 1992, Patricia packed in
her job at the advertising agency. The
following month, she was pregnant. Max
had struck again! Things definitely
appeared to be looking up when he was
offered a partnership with Fletcher's the
Estate Agents but it all went wrong when
Patricia suffered a miscarriage while acting
as guest speaker at a Round Table lunch.
She later set up in business with her old
boss Karyn Clark.

The spectre of Susannah was never far
away. She turned up with her new actor
boyfriend Andrew and announced that they
were taking Matthew and Emily to live in
the United States. Fearing that Andrew
would replace him in his children's affections, Max vowed to fight her all the way
and finished up going to Florida and
snatching them back. Susannah returned
home for the showdown. Patricia was away
in London on business. Susannah played on
his emotions, using the children as her
weapons and herself as bait. Max, who at
times displayed about as much backbone as
a slow-worm, surrendered meekly and they
went to bed. David Crosbie found out and,
after enjoying watching Max squirm, carried

*Peter Harrison consoles Diana Corkhill on the
stairs of number 7.*

out his threat to tell Patricia. She walked out
on him and moved into the Crosbies'
bungalow next door.

On 1 October 1993, the Farnhams' decree
absolute came through. Two weeks later,
they remarried. With the Farnhams, joy and
despair tended to go hand in hand. Early in
1994, Patricia fell pregnant once more. They
were both overjoyed – until she learned that
the baby would be Down's Syndrome.
Although given the chance to terminate the
pregnancy she and Max decided to go
ahead with the baby.

Patricia was eager to have the house
redecorated for the new arrival. She was
delighted with her distinctive choice of
wallpaper until she found out that the
Bankses had exactly the same design in their
box room! So she ripped it down. A
disgruntled Max had to start all over again.

Baby Alice was born on 19 August 1994.
By then, Patricia had come to terms with the
fact that her child would be Downs
Syndrome and just wanted people to treat
her and Max normally. Max was less adapt-
able. He was scared of the baby and avoided
her as much as possible, leaving for work
early and getting home late. He preferred to
immerse himself in the opening of his new
restaurant. When his partner in the venture,
Barry Grant, had disappeared (held against
his will at number 5), Max had been worried
that the deal would fall through. Patricia
had warned him not to trust Barry. But for
once, Max's faith was justified. The restaurant opened on 5 November 1994, with a
bang!

Under the Farnhams' occupation,
number 7 has earned the reputation of a
house of sin. Max slept there with Susannah;
Margaret climbed into bed with Derek,
Keith Rooney and Beth Jordache (although
not all at the same time); Diana Corkhill and
Peter Harrison went upstairs for an ill-fated
encounter; and Beth and Chris were caught
in a delicate position by David Crosbie.
Maybe they should put a red light in the
hallway and charge admission.

number 8

There was something ironic about the fact that Paul Collins should be living on the same Close as Bobby Grant. A year earlier, Paul resided in his big house on the Wirral while Bobby slummed it on a council estate. They were from different ends of the social scale. Their paths would never have crossed. Paul was no more likely to frequent working-men's clubs than Bobby was to attend a cheese and wine party. But circumstances had dictated that in this league of life, Paul would suffer relegation and Bobby would gain promotion. Suddenly they were playing in the same division. Paul did not enjoy the experience one bit.

Paul, his wife Annabelle (a former French teacher) and their teenage children Gordon and Lucy had always been used to the finer things in life. Paul was a well-paid production manager at a local refinery called Petrochem but the recession of the early 1980s hit the company hard, forcing widespread redundancies. The top tier was first for the chop and Paul found himself out of a job in his early fifties. It was a depressing position in which to be. Where on earth was he going to find another job at his age, especially one which paid so well?

Paul may have been out of touch in some other respects but his actions here were totally practical. There was no use hoping that a fairy godmother would come along with a job application form on the end of her wand – they had to face facts. Belts would have to be tightened and circumstances reduced. Instead of buying smoked salmon from the supermarket, Annabelle would have to settle for fish fingers . . . and go easy on the ketchup.

It was the reduction in circumstances which brought the Collins clan to 8 Brookside Close, a house barely half the size of their previous abode. And whereas their old neigbours had been captains of industry and golf club presidents, now they had the Grants. It took a lot of getting used to.

First impressions can be misleading but in this case, they weren't. As Paul and his family entered their new home, they found the door already open. Damon Grant and his cronies rushed past them. On exploring further, the Collinses discovered that the place was littered with cigarette stubs, there was graffiti sprayed on the bedroom walls and someone had stolen the toilet! Then, after returning from the weekly humiliation of signing on, Paul found that the entire Close had been burgled. What a welcome!

Both Gordon and Lucy had been educated privately but Paul could no longer afford to keep them both there. A decision had to be made. Lucy lost out. With his 'O' Levels coming up, computer-mad Gordon stayed put while Lucy had to mix with the 'oiks' at Brookside Comprehensive. The inmates took great pleasure in taunting her about her posh, middle-class accent. The jibes turned to bullying. They saw her as an easy target. But Lucy was made of sterner stuff. One thing she had learnt at private school was how to wield a mean hockey stick and when she took to her chief tormentor with one, she soon saw the bully off.

Paul had no rapport with his children or indeed with anyone else's. In his British Home Stores sweaters, he was a product of a different generation, one which couldn't or wouldn't understand modern phenomena such as pop music, fashion trends or fun. If only the kids of today showed the discipline which had been instilled in him in his army days. Bring back National Service, thought Paul . . . and the cat . . . and trial by ordeal.

At times, he bore an uncanny similarity to an early Victor Meldrew, the sort who, at the first hint of trouble, would dash off a

Paul and Annabelle Collins move into 8 Brookside Close.

letter to *The Times* about 'young Grant'. Annabelle was a different proposition altogether, much more amenable. It was her task to go round and appease the neighbours, to repair the damage Paul had caused – a bit like going round with a bucket and shovel after the horse.

She had plenty of practice in soothing troubled waters, beginning with the Grants after Paul had accused Damon of being responsible for everything from his missing toilet to starting the Falklands War. It was the start of a running feud.

Annabelle liked to involve herself in the community, even if it was not necessarily the community she would have chosen for herself. She stood bail for George Jackson and formed a local ratepayers' association, similar to the one she had been involved with on the Wirral. But her Tory instincts did prevent her from helping with the Women's Action Group during the strike at Fairbanks. She also served as election agent for an old friend, Robin Tate, prompting Paul to speculate that her relationship with Robin was more than just political. Ironically, when Robin later walked out on his wife Dorothy, there was similar speculation that Paul and Dorothy were up to

something. Both rumours were unfounded. Paul and Annabelle may not have had the perfect marriage but, for the time being, they were content enough with each other.

Paul was disillusioned at his inability to find a half-decent job. The chip on his shoulder had developed into a full sack of potatoes. To mark a full year of unemployment, Paul went for an interview at the Dole Office where it was suggested that he become a YOP's organiser. He was delighted to get back into a daily routine, to have a purpose in life, but was appalled at the irresponsible attitude of the youngsters on the scheme. Following some trouble with a trainee named Skelly, Paul quit and involved himself in something nearer his heart – a retraining programme for displaced middle management.

He could have done with a retraining programme for Lucy and Gordon, both of whom seemed to have picked up some of the natives' less desirable habits. To Paul's disgust, Lucy joined CND with her friend Janice Toumey and developed an alarming interest in Bobby Grant's workmate from Fairbanks, Jonah Jones. Skipping her French 'O' Level exam to picket a council meeting on behalf of CND, Lucy created a disturbance and was arrested. She escaped with a caution but the damage was done. Annabelle, in particular, found it impossible to come to terms with the fact that her daughter had been in trouble with the police. The only solution was for Lucy to be packed off to France with their friends, Gerard and Monique Dubois. Perhaps there, she might come to her senses.

Over 18 months later, in March 1985, Gordon followed suit. Annabelle returned home to find the house in disarray and £40 missing. Gordon's photography-mad girlfriend Cathy explained that she and Gordon had argued. Gordon had vanished into thin air, only to turn up in France where he was staying with Lucy. Then came the bombshell. Annabelle received a visit from Mrs Duncan, the mother of the head boy at Gordon's school, who confessed that she thought her son Christopher had been having a homosexual relationship with Gordon. Annabelle and Paul sat down and pondered: where had they gone wrong?

The news came at a time when Paul had just started to regain his dignity, having accepted the post of production manager with a subsidiary of Petrochem. Even that was not plain sailing, however, since it brought him into conflict with his old adversary Bobby Grant who was wearing his union hat. They clashed over rumours of redundancies and the awarding of a maintenance contract. Paul was then accused of taking a bribe of a year's food in return for awarding the contract. He managed to ride that particular storm.

The threat of redundancies did not go away. Paul had promised Bobby that there wouldn't be any so when the opposite proved to be the case and redundancy notices were issued at Petrochem, Bobby was round to confront Paul on the doorstep of number 8. Bobby was all beard and bluster. Paul, a man once again in charge of his destiny, deflated him with consummate ease. The subsequent strike divided the pair once more.

Annabelle was tiring of listening to Paul going on about industrial warfare. She had heard it all before. So, as well as taking up jogging, she decided to start a little catering business of her own from home and hired Carol Thompson as a cleaner. Annabelle soon let it be known that she was running a business and not a café. When Paul invited some Petrochem managers home for an important strategy meeting, she told him that she was far too busy with her catering commitments to rustle up sandwiches for his guests. Paul was peeved.

Annabelle had installed a freezer in the garage. Naturally, being Brookside Close, items started to go missing. Eventually, Carol caught Sinbad raiding the freezer. In return for not reporting him, she made him clean the Collinses' windows for nothing. Annabelle was impressed with Carol's handling of the situation. For the most part, Paul permitted Annabelle to run the business her way although he was dismayed to find that Harry Cross had only paid her £25 for preparing the funeral tea for Edna's send-off when it had actually cost £56. In business, there was no room for sentiment – especially where Harry Cross was concerned.

'James is leaving his wife. Can't you see, it's me he loves, not her. We're going to get married.'

– Lucy Collins

In the autumn of 1985, Lucy returned from France. She had certainly changed, apparently for the better. She seemed happier, more mature, more sophisticated. Yet there was a nagging doubt at the back of their minds that she was hiding something or someone, a suspicion fuelled when she rushed out on her birthday and arrived home very late. The cause of Lucy's behaviour turned out to be James Fleming. They had met over in France and he had promised to fix her up with an interview for a job as a translator back in Liverpool. She told Paul that the job was as good as hers but came home rejected. James partially redeemed himself by getting her a secretarial job at the office where he worked. She had expected more.

Lucy told her parents that she had a new boyfriend, news which immediately set wedding bells ringing in Annabelle's ears. James was invited round for dinner. It didn't take Paul and Annabelle long to work out that he was married.

When they broached the subject, Lucy merely confirmed James's marital status and bluntly told them to stop interfering. She had no intention of giving him up. A worried Paul thought it best to have it out with James man-to-man. He was prepared for a full-blooded row but was astonished to learn that James had tried to end the affair but Lucy would simply not let go. James had no desire to leave his wife.

Furious that James had been warned off, Lucy announced that she was going to move in with him. She insisted that James was about to leave his wife and refused to listen to Paul's diplomatic statements to the contrary. But James's attitude at work began to convince her that all was not well. He was distant, he seemed to be avoiding her. Being naturally impetuous, she tackled the problem head on and went round to James's

1 Jimmy Corkhill, the proud 'owner' of Kowboy Kutz.

...ccess corridor leading to flats above

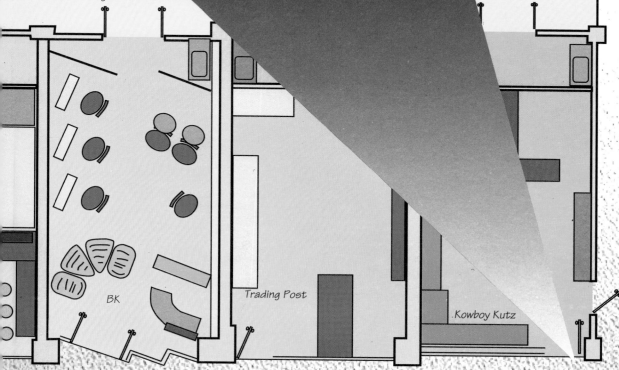

BK

Trading Post

Kowboy Kutz

3 Jimmy Corkhill's business venture was wound up in spectacular fashion.

Where Are They Now?

Caroline Choi returned to Hong Kong where she married last year.

Michael Choi and Alison Gregory split up within six months of going to the US. She now lives in California. He and daughter Jessica returned to Britain and he currently runs a practice in Kent.

Gordon Collins has furthered his career in the wine trade, and is hoping to have his first book, *Wine Tasting for Beginners,* published soon.

Lucy Collins has settled in France, living just outside Paris. Her relationships still don't last very long, due to her self-destruct mechanism. She still flits from job to job.

Paul and Annabelle Collins have stayed in the Lake District where they run a small, but very select, guest house. Annabelle's mother, Mona lives with them, but is now a widow. Gerald suffered a heart attack in 1992.

Billy and Sheila Corkhill are still living in Basingstoke. Claire is now nine and Billy is a self-employed electrician. Sheila works part-time as a school secretary. She thinks about and misses son Barry a lot, but never hears from him. She and Billy are currently going through a sticky patch, as rumours (as yet, unfounded) of Billy having an affair with a younger woman he was rewiring, reached Sheila's ear.

Diana Corkhill remains with her father in Liverpool. She has just started dating men again.

Doreen Corkhill lives alone in Bristol. She works in a shoe factory. She still regrets losing Billy and has never found anyone to really replace him.

Rod Corkhill is a security officer in Hull with a new girlfriend, Deena.

Tracy Corkhill runs one of the smartest hairdressing salons in the north-west. She has become very much a career girl, putting boyfriends second to her work. She avoids contacting her nan, Julia, in case she has to employ her.

Harry Cross continues to create havoc among the OAPs in St Helens. His new collection of garden gnomes is said to be the finest on Merseyside.

Owen and Sammy Daniels, with daughter, Louise, still rent their tiny flat, but hope, one day, to get a proper house of their own. Owen is working for a small company, (trying) to sell insurance and pension policies. Most evenings and weekends he studies, as he returned part-time to Further Education College. He wants to get into hotel and leisure management.

Jonathan Gordon-Davies lives in London with his wife Helen, two young children and a BMW.

Bobby Grant, split up from Susan Morgan, when he went off to work on the oil rigs. Colleagues say he's still there, involved in union activities. Susan and Bobby's son, Jack, wait for him to return.

Karen Grant works for a fashion magazine in London, a job which requires her to travel to Europe and the US on a regular basis. She shares a flat with another girl.

Pat Hancock went back to London to seek fame and fortune. But found the dole instead. He works in a wine bar, runs an aerobic class (ladies only) and attends, and fails, many auditions. But he's just waiting for the right part to come along.

Ralph and Lana Hardwick are still living happily in Las Vegas.

John and Barbara Harrison are living in Brighton where she is head teacher at the local comprehensive. He has finally adjusted to his role of house-husband and fills in some time as a prison visitor.

Peter Harrison has made a fresh start in Oxford where he has a steady girlfriend, Caroline.

Heather Haversham spent three years working in Ireland but now runs an accountancy practice in Derbyshire. She is in a long-term relationship with a local GP but refuses to marry him.

George & Marie Jackson moved from Leeds to Newcastle in 1988. In 1993, Little George was placed on probation for stealing cars.

Ellis Johnson very quickly got over being jilted by Marianne. He tells friends he was glad to be out of it. Mick hasn't heard anything from him, but believes he's living with a girl in London.

Michelle Jones stayed with the Jacksons for nine months, then got a flat of her own in Leeds. Three years ago, she married mechanic Dave Randall but within a month of the wedding, he was killed in an accident at work. She went to stay with George and Marie for a while but has now returned to Leeds, hoping to start afresh.

Brian Kennedy remains a guest of Her Majesty.

Angela Lambert is manager of a high class hair salon in Southport. She is having an affair with the owner who she hopes to settle down with, once he's divorced.

Sandra Maghie is now Sandra Hurrell. She and Dr Tony Hurrell have been married for six years and have three children. They live near Glasgow.

Alan and Samantha Partridge now live in Seattle, USA. After working in Kuwait for two years, they settled in America where he is a computer programmer with a multinational company. They have no children. He runs an ex-pats soccer team.

Geoff Rogers is in love. He met an older girl at the job centre – she was behind the counter actually, and within a week he had moved into her flat, in Bootle.

Lyn Rogers and her children live back with her mum. She occasionally baby sits Josh, for Bev and supplies a much-needed shoulder for her to cry on, when the latest fall out with Ron is announced. She avoids dating men, even though her mum keeps matchmaking for her.

George Webb was put in hospital for two months after being beaten up during a Nazi rally in the East End of London. The incident did little to alter his views.

house to tell his wife Penny about the affair. Lucy felt sure that once the wife knew, she would throw James out and he would come running to her. Instead it was Lucy who got thrown out. For James was there too and he left Lucy in no doubt as to where his loyalties lay. Lucy had been fun but it was all over now. A little girl lost, she rushed home and locked herself in the bathroom.

Subsequently sacked from her job, Lucy began stealing bottles of shampoo and, when she wasn't washing her hair, threw herself into a series of one-night stands. No man in Liverpool was safe. There were reports of parents advising their sons to go out in pairs as long as Lucy was on the loose. Paul and Annabelle were deeply concerned. Their only consolation was that whoever she took up with couldn't be worse than a married man. They were wrong. She took up with the dreaded Barry Grant and went off to France with him to sell videos.

Lucy was hardly out of the door before Paul learned that Petrochem had been taken over. He was made redundant. It hurt, particularly since his dismissal did not even warrant a phone call from Managing Director Brian Palmer. The only call he received was from the transport manager, asking for the company car to be returned. The whole episode left Paul feeling old and left out of the shop talk at the golf club.

But Paul did not remain idle for long. When Nicholas Black's son, Adam, was knocked down by a car, Paul was at the forefront of a campaign for a school crossing. He became a lollipop vigilante, committed to fighting the evil of cars. To make his point, he went out and bought a bicycle, even though he couldn't ride one. He also flatly refused to give Damon Grant driving lessons. Annabelle was worried that Paul's involvement in the road safety campaign would jeopardise her application to be a magistrate. Her fears were by no means groundless. The campaign leader, Kathleen Monaghan, organised a blockade, at which she and Paul were arrested. Despite her husband's reckless behaviour, Annabelle was accepted on to the bench.

In August 1986, gay Gordon returned home from France. Paul and Annabelle had hoped that their son's sexuality was just a silly phase he was going through and were overjoyed when he arrived with a girl, Cecile. It seemed that Gordon was back on the straight and narrow – until Cecile revealed that, over in France, Gordon had been her brother Pierre's lover.

Paul found it difficult to adjust to Gordon's homosexuality. At first, Paul was his usual dogmatic self but found himself defending his son after Carol Thompson, who had overheard their argument, announced she was quitting in case she caught AIDS from cleaning the Collinses' toilet. Gordon resumed his relationship with Christopher Duncan and invited him round to meet the folks. Paul was a bundle of nerves beforehand but he and Christopher got on surprisingly well, with a shared interest in cycling. Nevertheless, Paul was distinctly unnerved by the way in which the boys talked so openly about homosexuality. What Paul dreaded most was the neighbours finding out. He did not have long to wait. When the *Gay Times* was accidentally delivered to the Corkhills', Paul had to admit to a gobsmacked Billy that it was Gordon's.

Strangely, Paul became more relaxed now that everything was out in the open. Although he could never approve, he was no longer ashamed. To him, Gordon was just like any other son. If other people had a problem, that was their lookout for being so bigoted and small-minded. If not quite a new man, Paul was certainly in the throes of renovation.

Gordon got a job at a local supermarket and then partnered Chris in a furniture-restoration enterprise. Paul, meanwhile, had given a home to a puppy which he had rescued from drowning. He named it 'Lucky' although it was anything but good news for the neighbours. Sheila Grant complained that Lucky had fouled her path but worse was to follow when the refined Madge Richmond stepped in a pile of dog's mess. Lucky should have been in the doghouse – except that he wouldn't go anywhere near the kennel which Gordon had built. One night, Chris and Gordon went for a meal in town and fulfilled a lifetime's ambition by rushing out of the restaurant without paying. They then stole a car to get home. With Gordon at the wheel, they roared back into the Close . . . and killed Lucky.

Paul was heartbroken but his anguish turned to bitterness as he sought someone to blame. He convinced himself that Pat Hancock was responsible and, despite Gordon's pleading, took revenge by reporting Pat and Terry to the DHSS. All of a dither, Gordon felt obliged to tell Pat what his father had done. Pat marched round for the showdown with Paul and, in the argument which followed, Gordon finally owned up that it was he who had killed Lucky. Pat's response was to drape a banner proclaiming 'DHSS SPY' across the front of number 7 with a huge arrow pointing in the direction of the Collinses.

Pat Hancock's subtle way of pointing the finger at Paul Collins.

Between handing out stiff penalties to drunk drivers, Annabelle was becoming alarmed at the deteriorating health of her mother Mona. So Annabelle and Paul went up to Kendal and brought her back to the Close. Mona was a dotty old bird who lived up to her name. She took to Paul like a duck takes to oil. She got it into her confused head that Paul was a police spy and then accused him of trying to poison her. She was hard work. Even Annabelle was not immune and was most upset to hear Mona comparing her unfavourably with her son Teddy who lived on the Wirral. Paul thought if Teddy was Mr Wonderful, he could have her.

Any food prepared by Paul was immediately flushed down the loo by Mona. It cut out the middle person. In desperation, she wrote to Teddy about Paul but as she tottered out to post the letter, she fell into the black hole which had mysteriously appeared on the Close. Discovered by Ralph, she was carted off to hospital.

The only one Mona trusted was Gordon. They were two of a kind – outsiders in the claustrophobic world of 8 Brookside Close. Behind Annabelle's back, Mona persuaded Gordon to collect some things from her home in Kendal. Thinking 'Chris' was his girlfriend, 'Christine', Mona offered Gordon her wedding ring. Paul tried unsuccessfully to make Mona realise that Gordon was gay. He was wasting his time. She really was a few pages short of a pension book.

Chris saw Mona's house as a potential source of income and, unbeknown to Gordon and Mona, let it to Ralph for a holiday. When Ralph returned, he showed Paul and Annabelle his holiday snaps. They recognised the house and discovered that Chris had arranged Ralph's stay. They strongly suggested that Gordon should stop seeing Chris.

After five months, Paul and Annabelle put Mona in a home. It was for the best – even Mona, in one of her more rational moments, could see that. But when she came to stay at Brookside Close for Christmas, she insisted that the people at the home were trying to kill her. Here we go again, thought Paul.

Paul Collins had his hands full with Annabelle's mum, Mona.

As Mona sent letters complaining of ill-treatment, Annabelle and Gordon started to waver but Paul remained certain that she was imagining it all, just as she had with him. Immobilised following a motorbike accident during a swift sojourn in France, Gordon had difficulty getting in touch with Christopher. Having accidentally locked himself out of number 8, he asked Harry Cross whether he could use his phone to ring Chris. Harry, in a benevolent mood, agreed and Ralph returned home to hear what sounded like Gordon declaring his undying love for Harry! Of course, it was Gordon on the phone to Chris. When Chris came round to inspect Gordon's injuries – a state of affairs which caused him much amusement – Mona appeared out of the blue. She had run away from the home. Paul and Annabelle duly took her back but Mona's claims continued, ever more hysterical. They decided to see for themselves and when they arrived at the home, were shocked to find her covered in bruises. Matron explained away the injuries by saying that Mona had had an accident. They went away vaguely satisfied but Gordon and Chris took Mona's ramblings seriously. Now that Gordon had recovered, they decided to visit the home unannounced in order to check things out.

Their suspicions of ill-treatment were confirmed and they brought Mona back to Brookside. Paul still thought she was making it all up and proposed returning her to the home forthwith and apologising to Matron. However, Mona managed to remember the name of another woman, Mrs Harrison, who she claimed had also been ill-treated. Paul tracked Mrs Harrison down and reluctantly conceded that Mona had been telling the truth all along.

Mona, who proved to be far more enlightened about homosexuality than either Paul or Annabelle, considered selling her house and using the money to buy a place for Gordon and Chris. She would then move in with them. Paul thought it was a ridiculous idea and Annabelle became so irritated with all the sniping that she decided to get away for a few days – on a magistrates' course in Shrewsbury.

Although he'd had his share of run-ins with Damon Grant in the past, Paul was extremely upset to learn of his murder. What's more, his respite was short-lived since Geoff 'Growler' Rogers proved an admirable substitute. When Paul confiscated his football, Geoff and his pals plotted their revenge. They began by hoisting a chair onto the roof of Paul's house.

Soon Paul had more important things to occupy his mind than Geoff's pranks. Coming out of a gay club one night, Gordon and Chris were followed and taunted by a gang of thugs. A fight broke out, as a result of which Gordon and Chris were charged. The charges were later dropped. It didn't end there. The Collinses started to receive a series of threatening phone calls and a brick was hurled through the window, injuring Annabelle's fellow magistrate, Brian Lawrence. Then, after taking Mona to a new home, Paul and Annabelle returned to find number 8 daubed with anti-gay slogans. Annabelle took another offensive phone call from the queer bashers but the next time they rang, Paul deliberately provoked them, reasoning that they would either give up or come round. That way, he would be able to involve the police. All remained calm until a blazing car was dumped outside the house.

A major confrontation was looming. The mob had cut telephone lines to the Close but when they came looking for trouble, they were met by a band of angry residents. The queer bashers backed off. Even so, Paul ruled that Chris had to go. Gordon left too but within a couple of months, they had split up and Gordon moved back with mum and dad.

> *'You're having an affair, aren't you? With him! And I'm the last to know.'*
> – Paul Collins

Although he didn't know it at the time, Paul faced crisis on another, more unlikely, front. Annabelle and Brian Lawrence had been growing ever closer and the magistrates' course provided the perfect setting for a spot of extra-marital nookie. Paul had phoned her in Shrewsbury late at night to report Gordon's fracas with the police but had received no answer from her hotel room. He thought nothing more of it.

Back in Liverpool, the temperature between Annabelle and Brian reached boiling point. At every opportunity, they were locked in a passionate embrace like a pair of sex-starved rabbits. They had more secret meetings than MI5. Paul started to become a mite suspicious at Annabelle's frequent disappearing acts. She explained one absence by pretending that she had been out fixing a surprise birthday present for Paul. So when Paul stumbled across a hotel booking for the coming weekend, he assumed it was Annabelle's surprise present. In fact, she had booked it for herself and Brian. Hiding her disappointment, she changed the booking and summoned Brian while Paul was out. Inevitably, someone

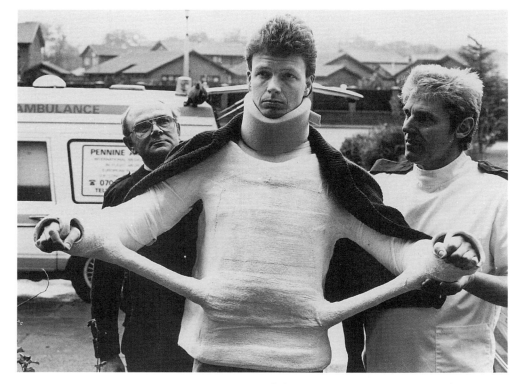

What the well-dressed motorcyclist is wearing. Gordon Collins demonstrates the latest in high fashion following his moped mishap.

had to catch them sooner or later and when Brian left, Sheila Grant spotted them kissing. Annabelle later attempted to explain but Sheila didn't want to get involved.

Gordon was going through a difficult period. He had been persuaded to go for an AIDS test and had no job to occupy his mind while he waited anxiously for the result. So Annabelle asked Brian to fix Gordon up with a job at his car showroom. The day after Gordon learned that the test result was negative, he started work as a car salesman. Annabelle's car went in for a service and Gordon wondered why the mechanics were sniggering. Rubbed into the dirt on the side of her car, he saw the words: THE BOSS'S BIT ON THE SIDE. Later, he too caught his mother kissing Brian. He realised that the car wasn't the only thing in the Collins house which went in for a good service from Brian.

Somehow Gordon had never seen his mother as a *femme fatale*. She seemed more the woolly cardigan type. He decided to confront Brian who calmly admitted that they were having an affair and that he had no intention of stopping. Gordon fought shy of relaying this information to either his

father or his mother. Annabelle feared that Gordon knew something but Brian reassured her.

For Christmas, Brian gave Annabelle an expensive ring. Paul found it and put two and two together. He invited Brian round for drinks on Christmas Day and challenged them about the affair. They confessed, at which point Brian slithered off, leaving Annabelle to face the music alone. Gordon, Mona and her new friend from the home, Gerald Fallon, arrived just in time to see Annabelle storm out of the house. Paul was a broken man. Dejectedly, he took down the Christmas decorations before going for a solitary walk. Christmas 1988 was one he would never forget.

Paul was upset that Gordon would not pack in his job. He felt that by not doing so, Gordon was condoning the affair. But Gordon was planning a far sweeter revenge on Brian Lawrence. He wanted to hit him where it would hurt most – in his wallet. So he stitched up Brian by selling his cars off at ridiculously low prices. Satisfied with his day's work, Gordon quit.

All in all, the first six months of 1989 brought better times for the Collinses. Annabelle quickly dropped Brian when she realised he was not interested in her problems with Paul and, after two months of sniping, she and Paul began to get back together. Gordon found another job as a car salesman and a new partner in wine merchant Ian, and in April, Mona married Gerald Fallon, and they moved in together in her house in the Lake District.

> *'I thought you didn't want to know about that side of my life.'*
> – Gordon Collins to father Paul

Of course, there were still hiccups. When Paul tried to reopen old wounds with Annabelle, after finding out that Sheila Grant had known about the affair, Gordon, unable to stand any more, walked out into the night. When he eventually returned, he told his parents he had been working on an AIDS helpline. Paul accused him of selfishness in not telling them where he was going, whereupon Gordon countered that he didn't think they were interested in such matters.

By then, Gordon had developed a taste for wine and was working for a wine merchant. He formed a friendship with a colleague, Judith, and together they unsuccessfully attempted to solve a wine fraud. She wanted more from the relationship but when he told her he was gay, they settled for friends.

Reunited, Paul and Annabelle involved themselves in voluntary work. Paul responded to a request from the Soldiers', Sailors' and Airmen's Families Association by helping out Maurice Walsh, a fellow Burma veteran. Annabelle took on a more onerous task, helping a street-wise young offender, Louise Mitchell, who suddenly turned up on her doorstep. She had run away from a children's home. To Paul's chagrin, Annabelle let her stay at number 8. It wasn't what he needed in his dotage. Louise confided to Annabelle that someone had been touching her at the home but refused to say who. It turned out to be her brother Gary.

Against all odds, Paul began to soften towards Louise and contemplated adopting her, even after discovering that she had stolen a wallet to give him for his birthday. The old 'hang 'em high' Paul would have had her marched off to the workhouse.

In April 1990, Lucy returned, the complete spoilt brat. She took an instant dislike to Louise. In a desperate effort to impress Lucy, Louise told her about Annabelle's affair with Brian. Paul felt betrayed. Louise ran off and was caught stealing from a supermarket. Paul and Annabelle decided against adoption after all.

Two months later, fed up with the constant bickering between Lucy and Gordon, the Collinses opted to move to the Lake District. Annabelle had been spending a great deal of time visiting her sick mother up there, so decided to go and help full-time. Lucy went to manage a restaurant in France while Gordon considered a business venture with Judith. She left him the key to her flat so that he could stay whenever he wanted.

While the house lay empty, the homeless Sinbad took up residence in the garden shed, a tenancy which ended when his primus stove caused the shed to catch fire.

At the end of September, the Dixons moved in. The Close would never be the same again. The sight of Ron's garish mobile shop, known affectionately (except by his neighbours) as the Moby, was enough to deter any alien invader. When England was

The Dixons have landed.

no.8

Annabelle and Brian pursued
their affair for over four months.
Paul never suspected a thing.

2
Annabelle arranged
a weekend away for
herself and Brian
but Paul stumbled
across the booking
and she was force
to change her plans.

Annabelle Collins' Affair

It was in 1988 that Annabelle Collins, bored with stick-in-the-mud husband, Paul, embarked on a wild fling with fellow magistrate Brian Lawrence. It began on a course in Shrewsbury and continued with a vengeance back in Liverpool.

Brian was a used-car dealer and, at Annabelle's request, gave a job to Gordon Collins, Annabelle and Paul's son. Soon Gordon discovered that Brian had been attending to his mum's bodywork as well as that of his used-cars and when Brian gave Annabelle a ring for Christmas, Paul finally got the message. He invited Brian round for drinks on Christmas Day and confronted the pair of them about the affair. They admitted it but when the going got tough Brian made his excuses and left. Annabelle started to realise that maybe she was better off with Paul after all.

upstairs

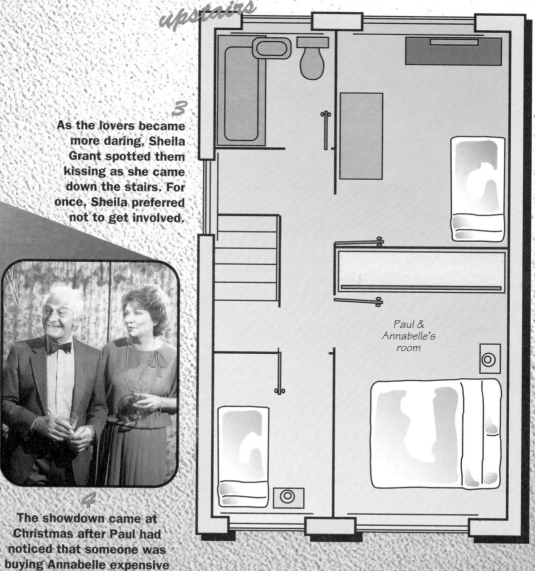

3
As the lovers became more daring, Sheila Grant spotted them kissing as she came down the stairs. For once, Sheila preferred not to get involved.

Paul & Annabelle's room

4
The showdown came at Christmas after Paul had noticed that someone was buying Annabelle expensive jewellery.

Jacqui Dixon and Keith Rooney look apprehensive before Mike's car race with Sinnott. Their fears were justified: Mike ended up in hospital.

described as 'a nation of shopkeepers', they weren't thinking of Ron Dixon. Full of working-class *bonhomie*, Ron had been married to Debbie (known to all as DD) for 18 years. He had worked in a factory in Kirkby for years but decided to follow Mrs Thatcher's advice and go self-employed. He bought the Moby with his redundancy payment. He was the life and soul of any party . . . and often the reason why people left early. Behind the wisecracks, he was a hard grafter, prepared to work all hours to support his family. He tended to be a bit set in his ways – to celebrate their anniversary, he had taken DD to the same restaurant every year.

Ron thought he knew DD inside out – indeed sometimes at the height of a religious rage, her face contorted to such an extent that it looked as though she was inside out. But, in truth, there was a lot about her that he didn't know for she had gone to great lengths to keep her past a secret. Her upbringing was shrouded in unhappiness. Both her parents died when she was 17. Her father succumbed to a terminal illness and her grief-stricken mother committed suicide shortly afterwards. At the time of the double tragedy, DD was a novice nun, having just left convent school, and the effect made her strongly question her faith. If there is a God, how can He let such awful things happen? So she turned her back on her beliefs and

went off in the opposite direction, becoming something of a wild child for the next eight months.

It was all an act, designed to cover up the sadness of losing both her parents and her faith. She couldn't play the part any longer and suffered a nervous breakdown, admitting herself voluntarily into a mental institution as an in-patient for 18 months. While in hospital, she became friendly with one of the cleaners, Maria Benson, and told her everything. Back in the outside world, Debbie began to rebuild her life. She met Ron but, fearing his reaction, invented a totally new past for herself. He only found out some 20 years later.

The event which sparked off the revelation was a tarot card reading at which Maria confided to DD that she had a fancy man. To cover for her friend, DD had to lie to Maria's husband, Charlie. But she could not bring herself to do it for long – she detested deceit in a marriage – and poured her heart out to Ron.

There were three younger Dixons. Mike, the eldest, was a strapping youth who made heads turn, notably Sammy Rogers and Margaret Clemence. He was fiercely protective towards his sister Jacqui. Finding her sick and frightened in her bedroom one night following a party, he discovered that a sixth-former at school, Sinnott, had given her some acid. He reacted by beating up Sinnott and was suspended. The bad feeling between the two lads festered. Sinnott caused Mike and Jacqui to be caught in possession of drugs (they escaped with a caution) and Mike took full revenge by spiking Sinnott's cola, as a result of which Sinnott hurled himself through a window.

Mike Dixon – just a singer in a rock 'n' roll band.

Still trying to prove he was top dog, Mike later challenged Sinnott to a daredevil car race for a £100 bet. Mike crashed and wound up in hospital but at least he and Sinnott agreed to call a truce.

At polytechnic, Mike furthered his musical ambitions and, encouraged by Vicky Lomas, took his band to play a gig there. It ended in disaster when his singer, Tina, doped-up by Sinnott, stripped off on stage. To prepare for the gig, Mike had bought a keyboard on hire purchase but soon struggled to keep up the repayments.

When she wasn't being cheeky to her parents, Jacqui Dixon was practising hard to get into the swimming team. Ron tried to instill some discipline into his kids and grounded them regularly. When he found that Jacqui had disobeyed him, he slapped her round the face. Their relationship remained frosty until Ron was forced to eat humble pie. Fortunately, it was not one he'd bought from the Moby.

Tony Dixon was a little horror straight from the pages of the *Beano*. On his seventh birthday, he drank half a bottle of Martini and had to have his stomach pumped. With his mates Togga and Benno, he wreaked havoc on the Close, making great capital out of his dad's feud with Max Farnham. He sent Max an unordered delivery of ten pizzas and Patricia 15 Valentine's cards.

An occasional caller to number 8 was Ron's wayward dad, Cyril, the apple of Julia Brogan's eye. He lived in a fantasy world, principally because he was a bigamist three

Jacqui Dixon, checking on the price of a decent pair of trainers.

times over. But he met his match in Julia. She was like a dog with a bone and bullied Cyril into getting engaged, or else she'd bury him! She invited half of Liverpool to the engagement party – in fact the only person who didn't turn up was Cyril himself! Julia never did get him up the aisle – he died at the end of 1991 from a massive heart attack.

Ron's great ambition in life was to own a proper shop instead of one on wheels. So when he heard about Brookside Parade, he was first in the queue to tackle owner Barry

Sisters, sisters, never were there such devoted sisters. Ron Dixon splits up the feuding Bev and Lyn.

Grant. Ron opened the Trading Post in October 1991 but the sacrifices needed to fund it created family conflict, particularly with daughter Jacqui who refused to be fobbed off with anything but the most expensive designer trainers.

'Someone's taking money out of the till. The question is who?'

— Ron Dixon

Owing to a misunderstanding, Ron found himself with two shop assistants – Jimmy's wife, Jackie Corkhill, and Julia Brogan. Unable to choose between the two, he had them working separate shifts. Mike, desperate for money to pay for his keyboard, began stealing from the till, first £10 then larger amounts. Ron accused the women of thieving from the till and they both walked out on him. They later returned but Mike framed Julia and Ron sacked her. On a slippery downward slope, Mike even resorted to stealing his late grandfather's war medals. Finding a pawn ticket in Mike's pocket, Ron eventually realised that it was his own son who had stolen both the till money and the medals. Apologising to Julia, who had earlier humiliated him down at the Legion, was not something Ron was relishing. And Julia milked the situation for all it was worth. To her, it was a clear case of 'defacation' of character!

With DD deranged over the Margaret and Derek affair, Ron sought refuge in the shop. Home was no place for the faint-hearted. He became concerned about

Jacqui's involvement with Darren Murphy, a member of a gang who had been vandalising the shopping area. Jacqui was with Darren and the gang when they broke into Manor Park Primary School one evening. Messing about with a lighter, Darren started a fire. The others ran off but Jacqui was trapped in the blazing classroom, only to be rescued in the nick of time by the passing Barry Grant. Ron's attempts to nail Darren resulted in a stolen car being dumped outside his house and then his shop window being smashed.

DD's relationship with Ron never recovered from the fact that he appeared to condone the romance between Margaret and Derek. He just liked to see two people being happy and that was why he loaned them the money to go away on holiday together. But DD, spurred on by the guilt from her own loss of faith as a teenager, saw things differently. When she found out about the loan, she walked out on Ron. She was back within a week but things were rarely the same again. After a lull in hostilities, Ron bridled at the way she helped Jacqui's friend Leanne Powell obtain an abortion without her parents' knowledge. He was also annoyed to find out that DD planned opening a florist's on the parade and had been saving up for years behind his back. How many more secrets was she hiding? In an attempt to patch things up, they went on a second honeymoon to Blackpool but DD was as cold as the cod fillets in Ron's shop freezer. And Blackpool was even colder.

Ron needed warmth and so, getting none from DD, turned the Trading Post into a little love-nest, first with Jackie Corkhill and then Lyn's sister Bev. When the back room door was shut, you could bet that Ron was up to more than stock-taking.

Bev made him feel young again. He went out and bought new clothes (for the fuller figure) and aftershave that was a step up from Brüt. Meanwhile, DD was sinking into depression, deepened by the discovery of her husband enjoying a lingering kiss with Bev. She went away to a convent to recuperate. She told the children that as soon as she was well enough to come home, she wanted Ron out of the house.

Having paid for the deposit on a flat for Bev, Ron began to get cold feet. Bev was only too willing to warm them up but Ron still felt something for DD. He couldn't bear hurting her. Bev was not a girl to be messed about and quickly found herself a new fella – Mike. Bev had no qualms about using Mike to satisfy her own carnal lust and to put Ron's nose well and truly out of joint. When she became pregnant, nobody could be sure whether the father was Ron or Mike . . . or indeed anybody else in the northern hemisphere. Not for the first time, father and son came to blows.

Bev wanted an abortion – she'd already had one when she was 14 – but Ron persuaded her that a baby was the icing on the cake for their relationship. It would bring them closer together. He now seemed resigned to losing DD. To all intents and purposes, their marriage was over.

Ron decided to install Bev in number 8, to the disgust of his own children and Bev's sister Lyn. When Jacqui burst in on Ron and Bev, she didn't mince words. She called Bev a slag and disowned her father. Later, she threw Bev's things out on to the Close. Ron arranged to decorate the flat above the Trading Post so that Bev could move in there, but that fell through when the money ran out. She hardly slept in the same bed two nights running – but then again, that was the story of her life.

Despite all the aggravation, Ron was happy with Bev and wanted the world to know it. He became a regular compère at the Legion but the laughter stopped at Frank and Lyn's wedding. DD was back by then but Ron hadn't plucked up the courage to tell her about Bev's pregnancy. At the wedding, she saw for herself and angrily attacked him. Tony joined in too. Ron slapped him. It would be the final memory Tony had of his father for on the way to the reception, the Rolls in which Tony was travelling crashed, killing Frank and leaving the boy in a coma.

Guilt-ridden Ron conducted a bedside vigil. He told Bev it was all her fault and that they were finished. DD was strangely conciliatory, telling him he had a responsibility to Bev's unborn child. Ron and Bev were reunited and, shortly before Tony died, she gave birth to baby Josh, on Christmas Day, also Ron's birthday. Ron moved out of number 8 and into Bev's old flat. They were a family at last. With such a strong-willed woman as Bev, there would always be conflict, such as when she flirted with the flash new compère at the Legion, Ray Piper, and proceeded to defeat Ron in a talent contest. You could hardly blame Ron for being upset – she had a voice which could peel paint.

But that was nothing to the furore which broke when, at DD's suggestion, tests were conducted to determine the identity of Josh's father. They revealed that it was Mike and not Ron. Bev tried to keep the results a secret but Ron found out. Not unnaturally, he was a mite peeved and stormed out of the flat, homeless at first, but eventually back to DD. More surprisingly, in view of all that had happened, DD welcomed him back with open arms. But Ron started to miss Bev and baby Josh . . . More changes were afoot at number 8 Brookside Close.

Ron and DD, united in grief at Tony's funeral.

number 9

Heather and Roger Huntington were Brookside's young professionals. She was everybody's favourite neighbour, an Irish accountancy undergraduate with a winning smile and a friendly word for everyone, be it Damon Grant or Harry Cross. As she drove off to her workplace, the firm of Hamilton Devereux, in her yellow Citroen 2CV, she seemed to have the world at her feet.

But Roger, a solicitor's clerk from Salford, was not satisfied. He had met Heather while they were both students at Liverpool University and although their marriage was still in its infancy, his parents were beginning to ask awkward questions regarding the continued absence of any patter of tiny feet. Heather preferred to immerse herself in her forthcoming final accountancy exams. Roger, who was used to getting his own way, began to feel neglected.

He had always been aware that other men found Heather irresistibly attractive but was nevertheless surprised when his boss, Derek Hobbs, made a pass at her at the Law Society Dinner. Heather did her best to defuse the situation but Hobbs persisted, sending her expensive presents and indicating that Roger's career could hinge on her co-operation.

Roger enjoyed the trappings of success – long lunches, expense accounts, business trips – and saw an affair with a wealthy, pretty client as another perk. Perhaps it was tax-deductible. He fell for Diane McAllister. The overnights became more frequent, partly because Hobbs wanted him out of the way so that he could mount his own fruitless pursuit of Heather.

When he was at home, the pressure of having two women on the go at the same time made Roger behave irrationally. He and Heather bickered relentlessly. One evening, she refused to collect him from

work. Walking home, he was run over and finished up in hospital with four broken ribs. Two months later, he stormed out of the house in a rage, ranting and raving about Heather's impulsive spending. When he returned, he slept on the sofa.

'You sod! Think I'm paranoid, do you? All in my mind, was it? I looked after you after that bloody operation of yours. You get out, Roger. Just get out. Go on, go to Diane. And while you're at it, you can take your bloody work with you!'
– Heather Huntington

In September 1983, Roger planned an extended business trip to Birmingham which would take in the sights of Diane. As a token of her appreciation, she gave him a tie pin which he only just remembered to take off before greeting Heather. While he was away on another 'business trip', Heather, tidying the house, stumbled across the tie pin in Roger's jacket. When he got back, she demanded to know who had given it to him. He tried to dodge the issue by going rugby training with Alan Partridge but Heather was waiting for him on his return. She accused him of having an affair. He lamely denied it but when she caught him on the phone to Diane, she threw him out.

Heather went to her parents' hotel in Northern Ireland to weigh up the situation; Roger went straight round to Diane's flat. Diane informed him that she was leaving for Barbados the next day. Roger was left out in the cold. He nearly warmed the house up with a fire but, after he had dozed off while leaving toast under the grill, the smell of burning alerted the Jacksons from next door just in time.

Over in Belfast, Heather listened to an old friend, Will Thurley, who advised her to make a go of life in England on her own.

Despite the efforts of Roger's father Syd, there was no hope of a reconciliation and it was Roger who was out.

Heather did not grieve. She passed her exams and invited her friend Polly to move in with her for a while. Instigating divorce proceedings, she reverted to her maiden name of Haversham but decided against selling the house. Instead she purchased Roger's half of the house from him.

Men continued to come and go in Heather's life. There was Dr Stuart Griffiths, to whom she was introduced at a party at the nurses' house, and used-car salesman Don Summerhill from whom she bought a Volkswagen Scirocco. She also got a reputation as a husband-stealer for just as she was about to cement the relationship with Don, his wife rang the doorbell. Don had told Heather he was divorced. He had been telling porkies!

Hot on the heels of Don came Tom Curzon, chairman of Curzon Communications, an expanding company on the brink of reaching the Stock Exchange. Heather was entrusted with the task of sifting through the company books prior to the flotation. No sooner had she started than she found herself dropped from the Curzon account. The reason? She had refused to mix business with pleasure by going out with Curzon Communications' chief accountant, Deaken Mathews. When Tom Curzon discovered what had been going on, he sacked Mathews and took Heather under his own wing.

Tom was Heather's kind of man: soft-spoken, charming and educated. He wasted no time in inviting her away for a weekend in Portugal. They got on famously. Back in England, they indulged in such romantic pursuits as crown green bowling and Heather was introduced to Tom's father, Jim. She liked him too. Things were getting serious. To celebrate Tom's birthday, he and Heather arranged to go out to dinner together but he rang up to cancel at the last minute. Heather decided to take his card down to the factory anyway, only to see him leaving with a young lady on his arm. Far from being a love rival, it was Tom's daughter, Rowena. Heather was hurt that Tom had never mentioned her before. She had endured a lifetime of men with secrets.

Tom said it was unimportant and asked Heather to marry him. They got as far as planning the wedding reception. She gave up her job in favour of one with Curzons but was disturbed to find that it was nothing more than a sinecure. She felt patronised, realising that Tom's ultimate vision was for her to relinquish her career altogether and have his babies. He wanted her as a pretty appendage, to impress clients, rather than as a woman in her own right. In many ways, he was Roger Mark II. Her mother, over for the happy event, urged Heather to think long and hard in case she made another mistake. Heather knew it would never work – she had come to value her independence. Although she still loved Tom, she called the wedding off.

Alone again and back in her old job at Hamilton Devereux, there were evenings when Heather began to consider whether independence was not an over-rated commodity. But she didn't have long to contemplate solitude. For, although she didn't know it at the time, she had just met her next husband.

Driving through the city one day, the MG Midget in front of her braked too quickly and Heather gently shunted into the back. The driver of the Midget was architect Nicholas Black. They exchanged addresses and a couple of weeks later, having heard nothing about the insurance claim, he called round. Heather gave him a cheque. The following night, he was back again. Heather, who was in the middle of decorating with Joyce, a friend from work, had put the wrong date on the cheque. Nick stayed to help with the decorating. Heather didn't give him the brush-off.

He seemed to be in his element, whistling while he worked. On his next visit, he said he would stay up all night to finish the painting. He told Heather to go to bed. Bemused, she agreed and when she got up in the morning, sure enough, Nick had gone, leaving behind an immaculately-decorated room. Heather was impressed.

Nick seemed like a breath of fresh air in her troubled life. He made her laugh by leaving cute little cartoons to say 'hello' or 'goodbye'. She needed cheering up since her new boss at work, Keith Tench, thought that her attractiveness was a liability to the company. The affair with Tom Curzon had gone against her. Tench undermined her in every way possible and put her on a small audit at a feminist print workshop. There she happened to meet Nick's lesbian ex-wife, Barbara. Nick also had three children. Heather got on well with the youngest, Adam, who shared a passion for cricket with Paul Collins. The other two, Ruth and Scott, were a different proposition. When he and Heather decided to tie the knot, Nick dreaded the reaction of Ruth and Scott. Ruth was particularly unpleasant, a self-centred would-be trendy who was intensely jealous of Heather's relationship with her dad. The

three were invited for dinner at Heather's one evening. Adam was delayed playing cricket but when his match finished early, he began to walk home. En route, he was knocked down by a car. Ruth and Scott seized the opportunity to blame Heather. Undeterred, in June 1986, Heather Haversham became Heather Black.

The best man at the wedding was Charlie Dawson, a laid-back ex-lecturer with an irritating habit of saying 'ciao'. The cake had barely been cut before Heather got an inkling that maybe there were still things she didn't know about Nick. It came from a chance remark by young Adam who told her that his father and Ruth kept secrets between them. Heather soon sensed that the secrets somehow related to Charlie.

Charlie and Nick went back a long way. Even with his new marital status, he would enter into conspiratorial huddles with Charlie. Heather half suspected they might be gay. She felt uncomfortable in Charlie's presence, not surprising since he possessed all the charm of the average leech. She told Nick she didn't care for his friend but Nick insisted that he was harmless.

Now that they were married, Heather expected Nick to give up his flat but he insisted on keeping it and, to her annoyance, allowed Charlie to move in. In her role of accountant, she started making an attempt to balance Nick's books but found that a lot of his expenditure was unaccounted for. With these concerns on her mind, she set off for a business trip to Hong

Heather and Nicholas Black on their wedding day. Nick's drug pushing pal Charlie (right) soon brought an untimely end to the union.

Kong. She hoped it would help her to see things in a clearer light and get her away from Ruth and Scott who had settled in with their father at number 9.

When Heather returned from the Orient, she found that Charlie had been staying at the house. Nick began jumping to attention whenever Charlie called. Heather knew she had to get to the bottom of it. Resenting the fact that Ruth was allowed to share the secret and she wasn't, Heather confronted Nick again about his relationship with Charlie. Nick had a little temper tantrum and drove off in a huff. Ruth eventually relented. She took Heather to the flat where they found Nick unconscious. He had overdosed on heroin. That was his secret – he and Charlie were heroin addicts. As Nick was carted off in an ambulance, Charlie disposed of the evidence. When Nick came round, he promised Heather he would never touch the stuff again. Heather wanted to believe him but Barbara advised her not to build her hopes up. Barbara was right to be cautious for, despite his vows to the contrary, Nick was soon back on heroin, supplied by the devious Charlie. Heather did everything she could to help him. Realising that the mysterious withdrawals were to pay pushers, she confiscated his cheque book but he retaliated by stealing her ruby pendant to fund his habit. He became impossible to live with.

Heather was at her wits' end. For advice she turned to Barry Grant whose ex-girlfriend Jane Smith had been an addict. Barry told her the only way out was to leave Nick. Sacked by the council after skipping a disciplinary hearing, Nick returned to number 9 as high as a kite. He tried to persuade Heather to take some heroin, so that she could understand, but she refused and asked him to leave.

Charlie came round looking for his buddy. He blamed Heather for Nick's disappearance and decline, claiming that Nick had coped until he met her. Then a policeman called with bad news. Nick had been found dead in Sefton Park. After taking heroin, he had fallen asleep on a park bench and died from hypothermia. Heather's marriage had lasted just six months.

She did not hang around. Leaving the keys with Barry, whom she pledged to silence, and without taking any of her belongings, she roared out of the Close in the dead of night and boarded a boat bound for Ireland. Everybody's favourite neighbour had done a runner without saying goodbye. And she was never to return to the house which held so many bitter memories.

Charlie continued to make a nuisance of himself. He wormed his way into Pat and Terry's for the night and asked if he could stay for Christmas. When they refused, he homed in on the Collinses. Just as he was about to get his feet under the table, Barry turned up and threw him out. Barry explained to Paul and Annabelle that Nick was dead and that Charlie had supplied him with heroin. It was one of Barry Grant's better deeds.

The contents of 9 Brookside Close were subsequently sold off by a solicitor and the following April, young solicitors Jonathan Gordon-Davies and Laura Wright moved in prior to getting married. A former public school boy, Jonathan hailed from London. He had met Laura at Liverpool University and, after qualifying, now worked for an established practice in the city centre. Although he loved Laura, he was less sure about Liverpool and always had a hankering to return south. Laura came from a working-class background but had striven to better herself. She was the personification of upward mobility and was that modern rarity – a solicitor with a conscience. Her parents were fiercely proud of her.

The strain of preparing for the wedding was beginning to tell on Jonathan and Laura, all the more so when Jonathan hurt his hand playing rugby and was therefore unable to finish the decorating. He feared that Laura's interfering father, Geoff, would be straight round with his brush. Jonathan, who was born to sulk, also moaned about the continued presence of Laura's younger sister, Joanne, who seemed to be making herself at home. Jonathan and Laura niggled at each other constantly. They were not the usual Brookside-style rows of swearing, smashed doors and hospital visits. Being professional people, they were more civilised, choosing such weapons as sarcasm, mixed metaphors and alliteration. And of course, they charged double time if the argument extended outside office hours.

With Jonathan's wealthy background and Laura's trappings of grandeur, the expectation was for a lavish wedding with a huge guest list. Fewer people were involved in the making of *Ben Hur* . . .

Ba' and Te' prepare for the latter's big day.

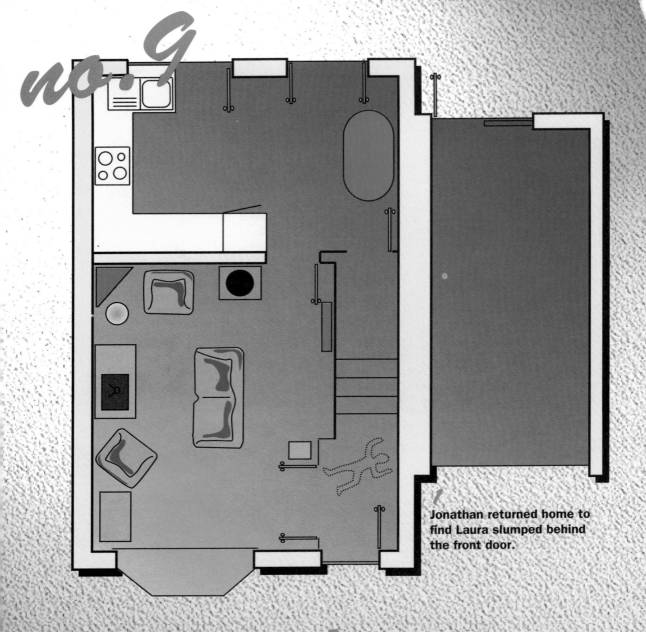

no. 9

1 Jonathan returned home to find Laura slumped behind the front door.

2 For three months Laura remained in hospital on a life-support machine. She was never to recover.

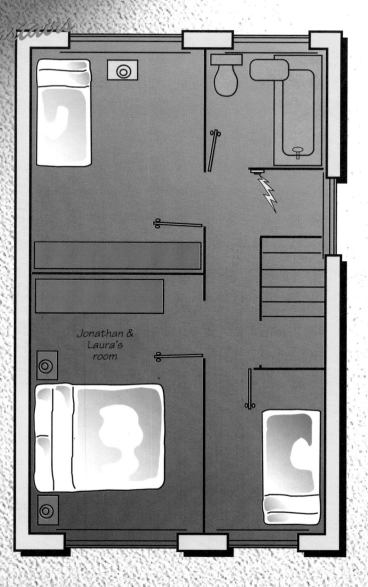

The Electrocution of Laura Gordon-Davies

Laura and Jonathan Gordon-Davies had only been married for two months when, alone in the house in October 1987, she stepped out of the shower, and went to switch on the light. She immediately received an almighty electric shock which sent her tumbling down to the front door.

As Laura lay unconscious in hospital, Jonathan too got a small shock from the light switch. He realised that the cause of the accident was Laura's interfering father Geoff Wright who was supposed to have fixed the switch. Instead he had fixed his own daughter. In January 1988, Laura was pronounced brain dead, but, inspite of accusations from the Wrights that he had something to do with her death, Jonathan remained tight-lipped about the whole business. He knew the truth would leave them devastated.

To complicate matters, Jonathan drove their Volvo into the vast hole which had just appeared on the Close. Laura was beginning to wonder whether Brookside Close was such a desirable address after all. She decided to move out of the house until after the wedding and devoted all her energies to a deportation case at work. It became so important to her that she announced that the wedding would have to be postponed. Jonathan felt he was playing second fiddle to her work. His bottom lip sagged even further.

On the day he should have been getting married, Jonathan found himself decorating, helped by Damon Grant who accidentally splashed paint on one of Jonathan's expensive jackets. Overall, Damon did a good job although his work was constantly criticised by Laura's father who was laying cork tiles in the kitchen.

After a few more crises, the wedding finally took place, a month behind schedule, in August 1987. The reception was held in a massive marquee in the garden of number 9 – indeed the marquee was so big that it overlapped onto the Corkhills'. Jonathan presented Laura with a slightly unusual present – a 40 foot high inflatable gorilla. Well, it made a change from toasters!

Sinbad welcomed the newlyweds by pinching tiles from their roof and then offering to fix it. He then tried the same ruse with the Corkhills' and the Collinses before Geoff Wright caught him out.

Geoff and Dorothy, Laura's parents, were a real pain. They were round at every opportunity. One day in October, Jonathan was irritated when he returned home to find Geoff in the house. He had come to repair a cracked light switch. Later, alone in the house, Laura switched on the light and received a mighty electric shock which sent her crashing down the stairs until she came to rest behind the front door.

With Laura still unconscious in hospital, Geoff tried to establish the cause of the accident. He and Dorothy were confident that their daughter would pull through but Jonathan was not so sure. For them, that attitude was bad enough but when Jonathan then allowed Terry Sullivan to move in as a lodger, it was tantamount to treason. It was as if he had written off Laura already. While Geoff Wright was blaming everyone else, it transpired that the one person at fault was himself. For when Jonathan also got a shock from the light switch, he realised that Geoff's shoddy handiwork was the cause of Laura's downfall. Although he must have been sorely tempted to ram this news down Geoff's throat, Jonathan, to his credit, refrained from doing so. In January 1988,

Laura was declared brain dead. Jonathan knew that, in order to protect the Wrights' feelings, he would have to lie at the inquest.

Terry had been chatting up Jonathan's secretary, Sue, but the courtship was interrupted when, to get away from it all, Jonathan persuaded Terry to go skiing in Austria. Fresh air and mountains were not exactly Terry's idea of a holiday – he was more at home with a crate of lager under Blackpool Tower. But despite the fact that he was as expert at skiing as Harry Cross was at hang-gliding, Terry entered into the spirit of the occasion, even borrowing £300 from Barry to buy some decent gear.

The heady Alpine air did little to lift the low cloud which still hung over Jonathan. He got depressed thinking of Laura – in truth, much as he had done when she was still alive. Terry meanwhile had struck up a friendship with a Canadian girl called Donna. To cheer up Jonathan, Donna got her pal Cheryl to make up a foursome. Gradually Jonathan started to thaw out and found that Cheryl was a good listener.

A few weeks later, the girls paid a surprise visit on Jonathan and Terry in Liverpool. Surly Sue was miffed to see them give Terry a very warm welcome. Terry had plenty of explaining to do, particularly since he had told Donna that he ran a fleet of taxis. She thought Sinbad was one of his drivers! Geoff Wright was also on the warpath. Appalled to find Donna and Cheryl staying at number 9, he threatened to order another inquest. In his grief, he had almost convinced himself that Jonathan had been involved in Laura's death. Jonathan was on the point of finally telling him the truth when Terry intervened.

Sue overcame her jealousy (anyway Donna had a steady boyfriend back in Canada) and she and Terry began to get their act together. Jonathan, meanwhile, was pining for Cheryl and, on a business trip to Canada, sought her out in Vancouver. He tracked her down at the university, only to discover that she too had a regular boyfriend, Deburau, whom she was due to marry now that his divorce had come through. However, Jonathan sensed that all was not lost when Cheryl expressed an interest in coming to the Manchester Business School. So, with Cheryl and Deburau were going through their wedding rehearsal, Jonathan marched into church and whisked her away. Although he returned to England alone, she followed shortly afterwards.

Accepted by the Manchester Business School, she moved in with Jonathan. For once, there seemed to be domestic bliss at

Peter Harrison catches Anna Wolska kerb-crawling.

number 9 with Terry announcing his engagement to Sue. But she started behaving strangely after bumping into an old boyfriend, Martin Howes, whom Jonathan had innocently invited for dinner. Terry was puzzled and told her she had to choose between him and Martin. After much deliberation, she opted for Terry. Jonathan nearly lost Cheryl too. She was having a bath when the Christmas tree caught light downstairs and a fire broke out. Terry rushed up and managed to rescue her but the pair were overcome by smoke. Luckily, the ambulance arrived just in time.

Cheryl urged Jonathan to redecorate – she thought it would help exorcise the ghost of Laura – but Jonathan was so inept that he was quickly relegated to the role of tea boy as Terry took charge. While Jonathan and colleague Sarah Townes contemplated setting up their own practice together, Sue dropped a bombshell to Cheryl. She was pregnant but Martin was the father, not Terry. To Cheryl's disbelief, Sue flatly refused to tell Terry the truth.

Sue went for an abortion but couldn't go through with it. Keeping the dark secret made her increasingly irascible. She rounded on Terry and Cheryl for no reason. Whatever Terry did was wrong. Finally,

during yet another blazing row, she blurted out that she was pregnant, carefully omitting the minor detail that Terry was not the father. Terry was over the proverbial moon. That afternoon, they drank a toast with Jonathan and Cheryl.

Terry: *Tell me who Danny's real father is.*
Sue: *You are.*
Terry: *Come off it. You've been lying to me for the last ten months and the nine months before that. You've been lying to me all that time. He's not mine, is he?*
Sue: *Course he is. Why should I be lying?*
Terry: *Cos you're a lying cow. He's not mine, is he?*
Sue: *Terry . . .*
Terry: *He's not mine, is he?*
Sue: *Terry, you're hurting me.*
Terry: *Not as much as you've hurt me, you lying slag. He's not mine, is he? How many more times you gonna lie to me? He's not mine, IS HE?*

The atmosphere in the house led Jonathan to guess that Martin was the father of Sue's baby. He told Cheryl that if Sue

no.9

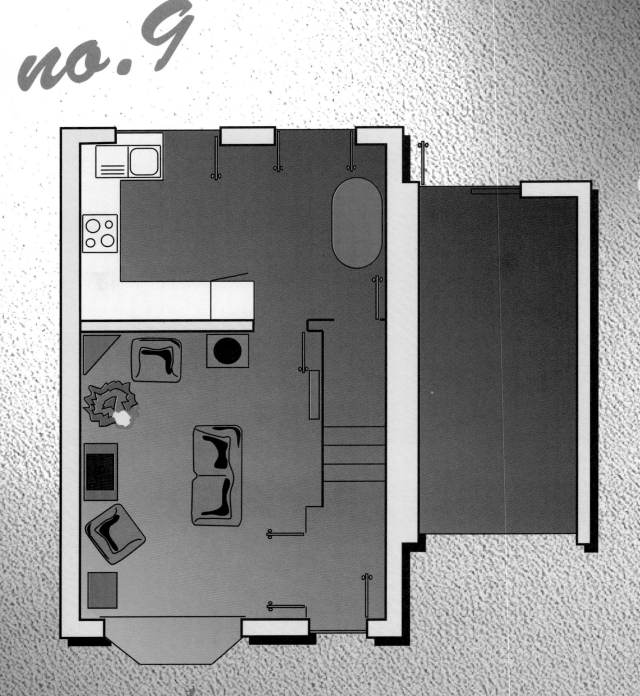

The fire started when the
Christmas tree burst into
flames.

Terry Sullivan: Hero of the Hour

Lawyer Jonathan Gordon-Davies had an unfortunate habit of never being in the house when he was needed. A year after Laura's demise, he and his new Canadian girlfriend, Cheryl Boyanowsky, had just returned home from spending Christmas with his parents when he was again absent as the Christmas tree in the lounge caught fire.

Cheryl, who was taking a bath at the time, was trapped upstairs but luckily Jonathan's other lodger, Terry Sullivan was on hand to effect a rescue. Both were overcome by smoke, but Terry recovered to complete the rescue. The emergency services arrived and ensured that serious damage was restricted to the wallpaper. Jonathan was so grateful that he promised Terry a roof over his head for life. He later changed the promise to a notice to quit. Terry obviously hadn't read the small print.

upstairs

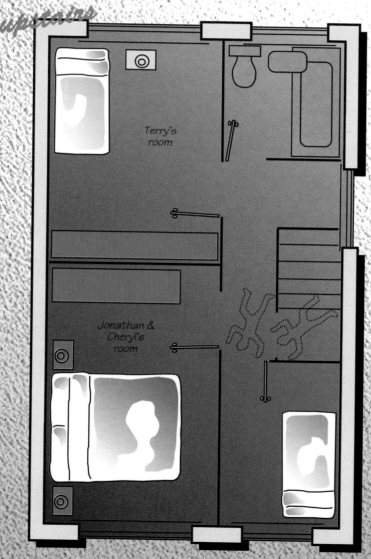

Terry's room

Jonathan & Cheryl's room

2

After hauling the unsuspecting Cheryl from the bath, both she and Terry were overcome by smoke but Terry recovered sufficiently to pull Cheryl to safety and become hero of the hour.

didn't tell Terry, he would. Cheryl could not bear the tension any longer and issued Jonathan with an ultimatum – they either move out together or she would go alone. Agreeing to rent the house to Terry and Sue, they arranged to view a waterfront flat but Jonathan was late, having been delayed by Coral, his new secretary, whose broad scouse accent offended his sensibilities. Tired of waiting and feeling that she came a poor second to his precious new practice, Cheryl packed her bags and fled to Canada.

Jonathan set out to follow her but was dissuaded by his business partner, Sarah. Sue's only concern was that Jonathan might not allow her and Terry to rent the house now. When she put him on the spot, an angry Jonathan told her that it was partly her fault that Cheryl had left. He also informed Sue that he knew the true parentage of her baby, and threatened to tell Terry. In the end, he couldn't bring himself to do it.

Jonathan had not given up on Cheryl and when a carrier firm arrived to take away her trunk, Jonathan noticed that it was to go to a flat in Manchester. He found her and begged her to return. He had finally bought a flat. Wearily, she agreed but made it clear that she was keeping her flat in Manchester as a base for her work. The relationship was doomed, however. In the wake of Terry and Sue's wedding, Jonathan started playing Happy Families. He talked about having children and eventually proposed to her. This was all too much for Cheryl and, in December 1989, she walked out of his life for good.

The Sullivans' start to married life was predictably tense. The heavily pregnant Sue needed all the rest she could get. Instead she got Barry Grant as a lodger.

Te' and Ba' went back a long way. After his mother's death, and his Dad's fondness for the bookies and the boozer, Terry had virtually been raised by Sheila Grant. As lads, he and Barry had been inseparable, involved in all manner of scrapes. Barry was always the leader with Terry following sheep-like. One of their most spectacular stunts had been when Barry decided to burn his Jaguar car in order to claim on the insurance. They had driven to Southport beach but didn't have sufficient petrol left to set fire to the car. Setting off for the nearest garage, they returned with a can, only to see the vehicle slowly sinking into the sands. It turned out to be the perfect method of disposing of the car – and nobody could point the finger at them. Sue soon wished that Barry had gone under with his car.

In September 1989, she gave birth to baby Danny. To ease her guilt, she told Terry that she wanted another baby but her plans had to be shelved temporarily when Danny was rushed to hospital with suspected meningitis. Although Danny recovered, Terry was still not keen when Sue declared that she wanted to go back to her old job with Jonathan. He was unhappy at the prospect of Danny being left with someone else all day.

The problems were piling up for Terry. Jonathan coldly announced that he was putting number 9 up for sale so that he could buy out Sarah. He gave Terry a lecture about his negative 'working-class attitude'. Terry was furious at the ease with which Jonathan had forgotten his promise after Terry had saved Cheryl's life: that Terry would always have a home to go to. Also, Sue's increasingly desperate attempts to get pregnant had proved fruitless, driving her into a state of depression. Terry decided to take a sperm test. The results showed that he could not father children. Taking Danny over to stay with Chrissy Rogers, he confronted Sue with the knowledge that he wasn't the baby's father. She brazenly tried to deny it but he wore her down and threw her out of the house. In a frenzy, he stripped the wallpaper in Danny's room and began burning Sue's belongings. He wanted to erase all memory of them both. Maliciously, Barry told him that Jonathan must be the father. When Jonathan returned from a trip to London, Terry attacked him. Under duress, Jonathan revealed that Martin Howes was Danny's father. Sue wanted to get back with Terry but he was in no mood for a reconciliation and snatched Danny. He brought him back unharmed a few days later and filed for divorce.

Terry's dad, Jack, called round and warned him against sinking as low as he had when Terry's mother died. Terry's hate began to subside and when Sue's mother was killed in an accident, he ended up providing a shoulder to cry on. Putting the divorce on hold, he invited her and Danny to move back into number 9. But nothing ever ran smoothly for poor Terry. No sooner had he got his family back than he was again faced with the prospect of losing the roof over his head. The restless Jonathan, while going for an interview with a Japanese firm, had met an attractive woman called Helen. He disbanded his partnership with his latest business associate, Viv, and moved to London with Helen. Before he went, he offered to sell Sue and Terry the house for a knock-down price of £40,000, giving them a mere six weeks to raise the deposit. Looking for somewhere to stay long-term, Barry lent them the £4,000 deposit and Sue took a job as a trainee legal executive.

*'If I was Terry and the operation was a
success, I wouldn't even waste the sperm
on you. See, if I was Terry, you'd be a
corpse now. You're not fit to be a mother.
You don't deserve Terry.'*
　　　　　– Barry Grant to Sue Sullivan

With Barry in residence, the temperature
between he and Sue reached boiling point.
She tried to be civil but he was openly
hostile. Sue knew the best way to get at
Barry was to be all lovey-dovey with his
mate Terry. He couldn't stand the competition, particularly after a consultant had told
Terry and Sue that it might be possible for
them to have another child. Terry went in
for an operation, as a result of which he was
pronounced fertile.

At last, Terry could become a father but
Sue had one more kick in the teeth for him.
With her new playmate Fran, she was
enjoying herself too much at work to give it
up now. She didn't care what Terry had
been through. She wanted to wait before
having another baby. Terry could hardly
believe his ears. To mark their second
wedding anniversary in August 1991, Terry
and Sue had a blazing row about her
delaying tactics. It finished with him
smashing all the plates and storming out of
the house. Barry, who had stunned Sue with
a lingering kiss a few weeks earlier, came
round to comfort her. They finished up
having sex on the sofa. Once again, Sue was
riddled with guilt and took out her frustration on a box of chocolates which Barry had
given her. She decided to try for a baby after
all. Terry was understandably mystified at
this sudden change of heart.

Incidentally, there was one other
passionate encounter at the Sullivans'
around this time. While the rest of the Close
were at the Farnhams' barbecue, Sammy
Rogers and Owen Daniels, the boy who had
wooed her since he was in the year above
her at Brookside Comprehensive, babysat
Danny and took advantage of the situation
on the sofa. But there was a sting in the tail
when Sammy fell pregnant.

Barry was not Sue's only admirer. At
work, she was being wooed by Graeme
Curtis, a divorced man who generally had
as much luck with women as Quasimodo.
He became obsessed with Sue, insisting on
offering her lifts to and from work. He stole
a scarf and a family photograph from her
desk. Fran later discovered the photo in
Graeme's desk. Terry and Danny had been
cut out. Sue told Graeme that unless he
stopped pestering her, she would report
him to the firm's senior partners. To get
away from him, she took a day off work,

telling Terry she was sick. She argued with
Barry, threatening to tell Terry, that Barry
had slept with her. Later that day, the
bodies of Sue and Danny Sullivan were
found at the foot of the scaffolding
adjoining the newly-constructed Brookside
Shopping Parade.

Terry was taken in for questioning. Terry
had been taken in all his life. He learned
that Sue had been pregnant and this time,
he had been the father. Terry couldn't
account for his movements – he had gone
out on a bender, convinced that Sue had
been having an affair with Graeme. When
Graeme turned up at the funeral, the police
had to drag Terry off him. Graeme was duly
charged with the double murder. He was
subsequently found guilty, a verdict which
caused him to commit suicide. But the real
killer was Barry Grant . . .

While Graeme was awaiting trial, Terry
began to go downhill considerably faster
than he ever had on the ski slopes of
Austria. Barry, the loyal friend, urged him
to sell the house. He did and on New Year's
Day 1992, Barbara and John Harrison
became the latest occupants of the 'House of
Hell'. It is not known whether the estate
agents made a virtue of the point that
within the previous five years, four residents of number 9 had met untimely deaths!

Barbara Harrison had moved to the Close
to take up her post as Deputy Head at
Brookside Comprehensive. It was a brave
woman who wished to live in the midst of
her pupils. Her husband John had taken
early retirement after suffering from
a late-onset of asthma. He and his brother
Hugh had closed down their engineering
firm which manufactured brass pins for
electrical plugs. John, the production
manager, had put his cash into savings
while Hugh, who was in charge of the financial side, bought a villa in Spain.

The Harrisons had moved to Liverpool
from Stamford in Lincolnshire and found
Brookside Close took a bit of getting used
to. Barbara was not only the wage earner
but very much the head of the house.
A domineering woman, she left John with
the distinct impression that if he messed up
the housework, he would be given lines or
even a detention. He was much more easy-
going but, forced to trail her around the
country, he felt like her lap-dog. Barred
from doing anything too physical, he found
it difficult to occupy his time. There was
only so much dusting to be done in a three-
bedroomed house.

They never really settled. True, they did
not get off to the best of starts when they
found themselves faced with a bill of

£70,000 to Customs and Excise because Hugh had been fiddling the VAT. The only way John could save his skin and his house was to shop his dishonest brother.

No sooner was that crisis averted than Barbara was the victim of a revenge attack by Darren Murphy and his gang whom she had caught stealing from school. They retaliated by hurling a brick through the Harrisons' smart conservatory. John decided to set up a neighbourhood watch scheme but when Frank Rogers and Ron Dixon became involved, it took on the guise of a vigilante patrol.

'I said no . . .'
– Diana Corkhill to Peter Harrison

In the middle of all this, the Harrisons' son Peter had arrived. At first every inch the rebellious son, he mellowed with the acquisition of a suit and an office job at Saffion Chemicals and started to look like the boy next door. He became friendly with Diana Corkhill and helped her learn to read. Sadly, he mis-read her feelings at a party in the Farnhams' house. She was going through a rough time with husband Rod and when she went upstairs in tears, Peter followed her. They kissed and cuddled and things got out of hand. The next thing, Diana was seen running from the bedroom in a highly

Eddie Banks shows his chest as he and Rosie move into number 9.

On the rebound from Beth, Margaret found comfort with Carl Banks.

agitated state. Peter found himself facing a charge of rape.

Coming on top of John's arrest for shoplifting (the culmination of increased tedium brought on by a severe asthma attack), the seemingly respectable Harrisons were earning a reputation for lawlessness.

Peter knew he was innocent but, apart from his parents, the only other person on the Close who believed him was Anna Wolska, the Farnhams' Polish nanny. Needless to say, there were plenty of comments from number 10 with Jimmy Corkhill upholding the family name. After one batch of insults, John took great pleasure in decking Jimmy. It seemed to give the normally mild-mannered John a taste for fisticuffs and at the trial, he came to blows with Julia Brogan who was also slagging off his son. It was all too much for Barbara. Just before Christmas 1992, she resigned from her job and told Peter that she and John were leaving for Brighton the following week. It had been a short stay, but at least they kept their garden tidy.

Not surprisingly, Peter felt that his parents had deserted him in his hour of need, particularly when hate mail began to arrive through the letterbox. It was sent to the wrong address. He was found not guilty.

John had told Peter he could stay on in number 9 until it was sold and in the meantime he took in all manner of waifs and strays: first Anna, booted out by Patricia Farnham, and then Mike Dixon and his mate Keith Rooney. Anna fancied Peter, seeing him as a solution to her problem – for she was an illegal immigrant and needed a husband if she was to be allowed to stay in Britain. But although Peter was attracted to her, he could not think about a relationship with any woman so soon after being accused of rape by a girl he trusted. And he was not prepared to enter into a marriage of convenience. With no job, Anna was desperate for rent money. She turned to prostitution. When Peter discovered what she was up to, he was disgusted.

Peter knew he could never live down the rape case while he was living on the Close. At one point, newcomer Beth Jordache became friendly with him – until Jimmy Corkhill told her all about the trial. Jimmy started a terror campaign designed to drive Peter from the Close. Peter couldn't be bothered to fight it and decided to return to Oxford (where he had been a student) and where he would not be subjected to cries of 'Rapist!'.

In March 1994, Eddie and Rosie Banks became the new owners of 9 Brookside Close. They had been interested in the Jordaches' but decided that number 9 was a safer bet. They obviously knew nothing of its history.

'They put a brick through the window, made threatening phone calls, tied him to a wheelchair in the street. What am I supposed to do? I can't even protect me own son.'

– Eddie Banks

Factory worker Eddie's proudest possessions were his Harley-Davidson motorbike and the coveted 'Bully' which he won three years earlier on the TV darts game show 'Bullseye'. Actually they won a speedboat, but sold it to buy the bike of Eddie's dreams. Super, smashing, thought Eddie. He and his traffic warden wife, Rosie (who later formed her own darts team, the Brookside Belles), had met when they were both in the Territorial Army. They had two sons, the eldest, Carl, had walked out on the army and his wife to flirt with Margaret Clemence. The romance was nipped in the bud when Carl's wife Sarah turned up with their baby daughter Rebecca. Margaret hadn't known he was married and Eddie and Rosie hadn't known he was a deserter. Carl was led away by two policemen and subsequently kicked out of the army.

Soon, the family were receiving ominous threats – hate mail, phone calls, a brick through the window. Maybe the residents objected to having a traffic warden living on the Close . . .

Eddie and Rosie were living in fear. The cause was their younger son Lee. He had spent the previous two years in a young offenders' institution after being convicted of joyriding, an incident which had left a young girl in a wheelchair for life. The Bankses had been forced to move from their previous address, the strain having been so great that they actually split up for six months. They had been hoping to make a fresh start in Brookside Close but the girl's family, the Kershaws, who had vowed that Lee would never rest in peace, had tracked them down.

Lee found it difficult to adjust to family life. He knew he was a target. The crunch came when he was snatched on his way home from Brookside Comprehensive. A

Eddie and Rosie discover son Lee dumped on the Close, with 'joyrider' scrawled across his forehead.

van dumped him on the Close, trussed up in a wheelchair, with the word 'joyrider' marked on his head. Eddie and Rosie whisked him indoors while the neighbours looked on in amazement. Even by Brookside standards, this was pretty unusual behaviour. Something had to be done. Led by Rosie and her larger-than-life sister Mo, the Bankses went round to have it out once and for all with the Kershaws. After a bout of jostling and spitting and an injury to Mick Johnson (who had gone along for the ride), a truce of sorts was reached between the two fathers.

As if they hadn't enough on their plate, the Bankses were also paid a visit by friendly neighbourhood burglar, Jimmy Corkhill, desperate for cash to feed his drug addiction. Returning home unexpectedly, Eddie caught him in the act. Jimmy's time was up.

In the summer, Carl moved out of the barracks and back into number 9 with Sarah and Rebecca. But he was only doing it to please his parents – he knew that he had married too young. He carried on seeing other girls, particularly Jacqui Dixon, but when threatened by wife Sarah that he could lose his daughter Rebecca for good, he tried harder to settle down. However, his mum Rosie started to fall out with Sarah, and, by trying to take Rebecca away from Sarah, forced her to leave and go back to her parents in Reading. Dad, Eddie, pushed Carl into finding a job to keep up maintenance payments for their grand-daughter. Carl responded by pinching Sinbad's window round and chamois leather. Window wars ensued until Sinbad took steps – well, actually Carl's ladders. Eddie, a strong trade unionist, had a fight of his own, when he found himself up against his new Personnel Manager, Marianne Dwyer, Mick's fiancée. The company, Litrotech, wanted more cuts than Jack the Ripper. Marianne was the girl to do it. Eddie was the guy to stop it . . .

With four deaths, a couple of fires, bricks through windows, a rape charge and countless broken relationships, number 9 has fully justified its reputation as the Close's 'House of Hell'.

Rosie's sister, Michelin Mo, wades in with Mick Johnson as the Banks' feud with the Kershaws gets out of hand.

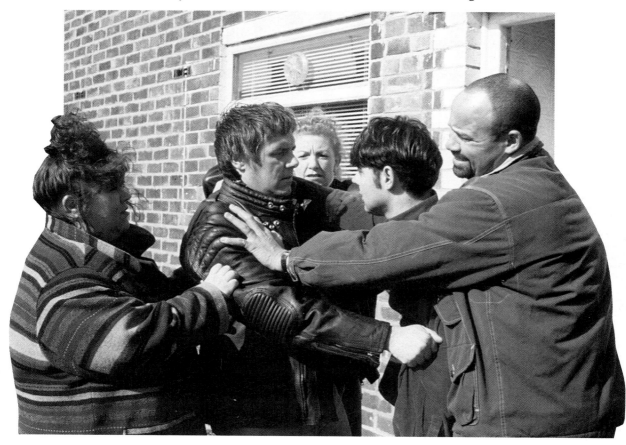

number 10

Per square yard, the garden of 10 Brookside Close has seen more blood-shed and strife over the years than Culloden. A body under the patio, cars being driven recklessly over the lawn, punch-ups – they have all taken place on this small patch of land. And it all began with 13 greasy cookers.

They were the property of Gavin Taylor, a would-be entrepreneur who, with wife Petra, was the first resident of number 10. Gavin was a graduate of the Del Boy school of business, buying and selling at a profit. That he was able to drive a brand new silver BMW was testimony to his expertise although the legend 'Gav and Pet' embla-zoned across the top of the windscreen said more about his character.

The cookers arrived before the Taylors. Roger Huntington, in particular, took great exception to the cooker mountain which proved such a feature of the garden next door. Then the Taylors arrived – not in a conventional furniture van but in a large frozen meat truck and another lorry with yet more cookers. When burglars hit the entire Close, Roger was peeved that they chose to leave Gavin's cookers behind. When Roger asked Gavin about the cookers, Gavin asked him about his sex life. Roger decided to fire off a letter to the City Planning Officer and Gavin was given a week to get rid of his merchandise. Gavin retaliated by erecting a hideous, multi-coloured shed made out of old doors. It was the sort of architectural feature which would inspire Ron Dixon many years later.

Petra, who worked as a typist at an insur-ance office, was not a happy lady. Not only did she disapprove of Gavin's business activities but she was desperate for a baby. Gavin appeared unwilling and unable to oblige and came to resent the slur on his manhood. The marriage became increas-ingly strained until one day in February 1983, Petra went upstairs and found Gavin dead in bed. The Close had claimed its first victim. He had suffered a brain haemor-rhage at the age of 26. Ironically, Petra then learned that she was pregnant.

Petra was distraught. Barry Grant, never slow to capitalise on another's misfortune, muscled his way into her affections, amidst rumours that he could be the father of her unborn baby. He had already carried out a number of jobs on the house while Gavin was still alive, including knocking down the dividing wall between the kitchen and the lounge. He now planned to demolish Petra's resistance. They sneaked off together to the Isle of Man for the TT races but on the boat trip back, Petra began to feel unwell and suffered a miscarriage. Barry could not even be bothered to visit her in hospital, an attitude which further infuriated Petra's pit-bull terrier of a sister, Marie Jackson. She left Barry in no doubt that she blamed him for Petra's miscarriage.

Despite the advice of her elder sister, Petra continued seeing Barry. But it was a rocky relationship with Petra steadily sinking into depression. Their arguments became more heated. When Barry refused to help with the decorating, half of Liverpool must have heard the subsequent row. Barry stormed off the Close, reminding Petra of her final argument with Gavin. Petra was haunted by the memory of Gavin. While looking at new cars, she saw a man standing beside a BMW. She thought it was Gavin and ran over to him. Realising her mistake, she rushed off down the road in tears. Barry could only take so much and, helping

The love that dare not speak its name. Beth Jordache shows her true feelings for Margaret.

himself to money Sheila had collected for a kidney fund, waltzed off to London.

Petra was unable to cope with life. When a jolly stranger chatted her up in the pub, she rushed out hysterically. A trip to the supermarket ended with the manageress having to comfort her and arrange for her to be taken home. Her younger sister, Michelle Jones, tried to soothe the wounds but to no avail. In August 1983, she packed a case and left home, leaving no clue as to her whereabouts. The police soon found her car – but there was no sign of Petra. A few weeks later, Karen Grant thought she had spotted Petra in St Helens but when Barry, back from London, drove over to investigate, it proved to be another case of mistaken identity.

Marie Jackson did her best to keep things ticking over. After all, she had looked after younger sisters Petra and Michelle since their mother died when Marie was 12. The sisters' father, Davy Jones, had been no help. He was a drunken old seadog who came and went as he pleased. With their own house being refurbished by the council, Marie decided to move her family into number 10 with Michelle. And so fireman George Jackson and the twins, Gary and Little George, arrived on the Close.

Marie was not one to give up on a cause, no matter how hopeless it appeared. She tried to use her psychic powers in an unsuccessful bid to trace Petra and then placed an advert in a newspaper. She then announced that she was setting a place at the Christmas dinner table for Petra and, for a moment, it seemed that her optimism might be rewarded. They received a Christmas card from Petra (with smudged postmark) and cheques were cashed in Petra's name in Southport. At least they knew she was still alive. But not for long. On 25 January 1984, Marie woke up from a bad dream. Later that day, the police called to say they had found a body in the room of a North Wales hotel. It was Petra. She had committed suicide.

In the aftermath of yet another slanging match with Sheila Grant (who saw it as her duty to protect Barry from Marie's vitriol), Marie began to wonder whether she should stay at number 10 now that their own house was once more fit for habitation. After only a few months, Brookside Close already held too many bad memories. When in doubt, she turned to a clairvoyant. This one told her to stay.

The wayward Davy Jones had different ideas, however. Arriving on the doorstep out of the blue, the first time she had seen him in years, he informed Marie that since Petra left no will and he was the next of kin, the house was rightfully his. He attempted

George Jackson stands in the dock.

to throw them out, only to be stopped in his tracks by the revelation that there was indeed a will. The house and £2,500 a year went to Marie while Michelle was promised an annual sum of £7,500. Davy skulked off in an alcoholic haze, pausing only to lift Michelle's catalogue money. It was a small price to pay to be rid of him.

With her new-found wealth, Marie considered getting the tearaway twins a place at a private school but even the flashing of pound signs could not persuade the headmaster to accept those two. It would have been like letting a pair of wolves share an enclosure with a flock of sheep. Meanwhile, Michelle, planning a career as a beautician, furthered her romance with Terry Sullivan who then lived on the local housing estate. She probably figured that if she could make Terry look presentable, she could achieve anything. Because of his friendship with Barry, Marie mistrusted Terry. She thought he was after only one thing – Michelle's money. But when she found a pair of Terry's underpants in Michelle's bed one morning, Marie realised he was after more than one thing.

Like many heroes, fireman George was an unassuming man, content with a pint and a pub quiz down at The Swan. After putting out a particularly tricky warehouse fire one day, he called in at The Swan straight from work, and began relaying the complexities of the blaze to Victor, henchman of budgie-breeding villain

Tommy McArdle. Innocently, George drew a plan of the warehouse on a napkin. The next thing he knew the warehouse had been broken into, with thousands of pounds of cigarettes and spirits taken, and he had been arrested for the burglary. Victor had covered his own tracks by demanding an alibi for that afternoon from Barry and Terry. They knew only too well that to refuse any associate of Tommy McArdle would have seriously damaged their health.

Against Paul's wishes, Annabelle Collins stood bail for George. Free from custody, he foolishly tried to reason with Tommy McArdle in The Swan, pleading with him for help. McArdle took exception to having his quiet drink interrupted and George had to be helped out of the pub following a beating. Later, he bumped into McArdle in the street. The mini-Kray told him not to make a fuss if he got sent down – he would look after George's family.

To escape the tension, Marie and George went for a day out in the park. Whilst there, George saved a young boy from drowning in the lake. He was hailed a hero – but it was short-lived since he had to get back home to sign on at the police station.

The rescue seemed to give George fresh heart. On the morning of the trial, he cut himself shaving and got blood on his shirt. Annabelle lent him one of Paul's. The superstitious Marie was sure it was a good omen – Paul had worn it to a successful interview – and the day's horoscope seemed promising too. But after pleading not guilty, George was soon in the mire. He was a nervous witness, easily confused by the prosecution. Barry and Terry finally realised that they had to help George and tried to do a deal with the police implicating McArdle. It was all too little, too late. George got 18 months and Barry and Terry got a sound beating from McArdle, Terry winding up in intensive care.

Marie was not finished yet and, with the support of ambitious young journalist Rick Sexton, launched the 'Free George Jackson' campaign. She organised a petition which she delivered to 10 Downing Street and when a government minister came to Liverpool, she disrupted the visit by daubing 'Free George Jackson' on the runway at Speke Airport. Tommy McArdle was none too pleased with the campaign. He issued threats in Marie's direction, culminating in a brick through her window. Marie began to wilt. There were other considerations too. The twins, taunted at school, had been in trouble for fighting and then Little George was accidentally shot in the eye with a stray air gun pellet while

playing in the woods. At least, Marie hoped it was an accident. The campaign was getting nowhere fast and so, reluctantly, she decided to call it a day. For once in her life, Marie Jackson was beaten.

George was switched to a prison near Leeds and Marie decided to move to Yorkshire so that she and the twins could visit him more regularly. The house was put up for sale and, in April 1985, Marie and the boys left the Close on the very day of Claire Grant's christening. Marie's parting gift was to give Sheila a silver locket for Claire. She was prepared to forgive and forget.

Before George's arrest, Michelle had put £2,000 into Barry and Terry's new tool-hire business. Terry in turn asked her to marry him and, with their matching perms, they moved into a flat together. Now, with number 10 temporarily vacant, they took up residence there. It was a fatal move. With no need to work (thanks to Petra's endowment), Michelle was bored. She took up dance classes and promptly fell for her instructor, Richard de Saville, a man better known to Terry as ex-brickie Albert Duff. While Terry suspected that Michelle was tripping the light fantastic between the sheets with Richard, she was curious about a secretive new job Terry had landed. It was, in fact, working at one of Tommy McArdle's clubs but he hadn't the courage to tell her. There was an air of mutual mistrust. Then one day, Terry returned home early and caught Michelle taking lessons from Richard in bed. Richard made his excuses and left while Michelle begged Terry for another

Billy and Jimmy contemplate the beauty of Barry Grant's arch at number 10.

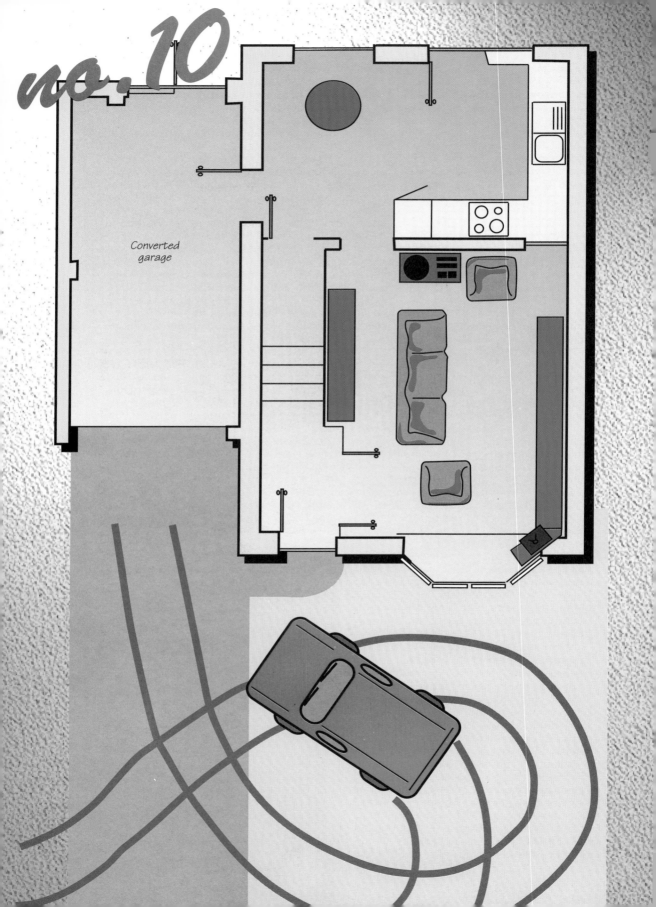

no. 10

Converted
garage

Billy Corkhill's Drive-in

By June 1987, Billy Corkhill was at his wit's end. With no money and no job, he had been steadily reaching boiling point since catching Pat Hancock brazenly driving his van over the front lawn of number 10 to avoid a mysterious hole in the road. So when wife Doreen confessed to having been tempted to sleep with her dentist boss Howman for money and then showed Billy a repossession letter from the building society, he finally snapped.

Climbing into his car, Billy drove frantically round and round the Close, leaving a trail of tyre marks across everyone's lawns. In some cases, it was an improvement. Harry Cross came over to complain, but sensing that Billy's brain was not at home, thought better of it.

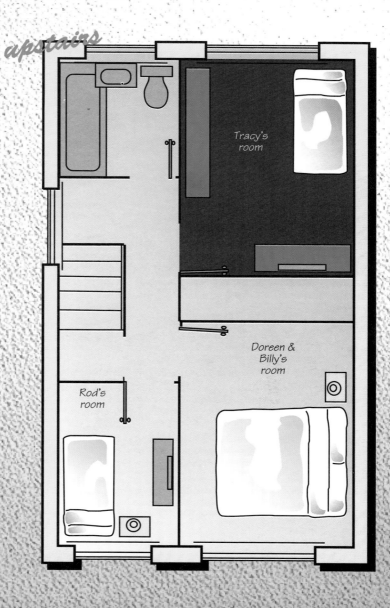

upstairs

Tracy's room

Doreen & Billy's room

Rod's room

chance. He wouldn't hear of it and hurled their double mattress out of the bedroom window, butchering it with a carving knife. Michelle took the hint, thinking it was for the best if she joined sister Marie in Leeds.

The house remained empty for three months until, in September 1985, the Corkhills hit the Close. Like the Grants, Billy and Doreen Corkhill had moved to Brookside from the nearby council estate. They couldn't really afford a house of their own but Billy, who was prone to letting his heart rule his head, thought she deserved better. And from the moment Billy drove onto the Close in his rusty old Datsun, the other residents thought they deserved better than having the Corkhills as neighbours.

Billy worked as an electrician with a local firm, Pollocks. The Corkhills were a notorious Liverpool family. Eldest brother Frankie was a local hood, murdered in a gangland vendetta, while Jimmy was king of the knock-off. Only Billy had managed to stay on the right side of the law – just. Doreen's mother, Julia Brogan, was eager to reveal details of the family history to Ralph Hardwick the moment she set foot on the Close. Doreen (Billy always called her Doe – 'They do Doe, don't dey, Doe?') was a dentist's receptionist who aspired to a higher standard of living. She was impressed to find that she was suddenly living next door to an accountant. Their teenage son Rod, hard-working and quiet, wanted to be a policeman while daughter Tracy, lazy and surly, had visions of becoming a model. Rod's support of Everton set up a friendly rivalry with Damon Grant who was a Liverpool fan. Rod even persuaded Tracy to swap rooms so that he could have the front bedroom and put up football posters to compete with Damon across the road.

When they moved into number 10, the Corkhills found that all of Terry's possessions were still there. Not one to stand on ceremony, Billy promptly dumped the lot out on the lawn. Once more, that patch of land was used as a dumping ground. Just about the only thing never to be put on it was a lawn mower.

One thing the Corkhills excelled at was operating fiddles, the electricity meter being a speciality. But when Billy forgot to unfix the 'leccy' at his mother-in-law's, Julia wound up with a heavy fine. Billy also fell foul of Paul and Annabelle Collins for putting large white shutters on the outside of the house. The Collinses thought that the shutters contravened the conditions of the ground lease. Billy didn't believe in things like planning permission.

With money at its tightest immediately after the move, Billy was reluctant to allow Tracy to go on a school skiing trip to Switzerland. But as ever, he backed down. He knew she'd only sulk for months on end otherwise. Tracy's principal motive for wanting to go was to pursue her young geography teacher, Peter Montague, on whom she had developed a schoolgirl crush. Naively, Montague responded in kind and when the party returned, the gossip was all over the school. Seeing graffiti on the toilet wall proclaiming 'TRACY CORKHILL GAVE MONTY A SWISS ROLL', Rod upheld what was left of his sister's virtue by attacking the teacher. He was suspended from school.

The Corkhills were mystified by Rod's uncharacteristic outburst until Julia, who had been an unwelcome guest in the house since her electricity had been cut off, revealed that she saw a love letter from Tracy to someone called Peter. Putting two and two together, Billy and Doe sat down and discussed the matter calmly and rationally. Then Billy went to the school and thumped Montague! For fear of dragging Tracy's good name through the mud, Billy would not tell the court the reason behind the assault. He received a three-month sentence, suspended for a year. But as a result of the publicity surrounding the case, he was sacked by Pollocks, a particularly harsh decision since he had defiantly crossed picket lines during a strike there, a move which had brought him into conflict with union activist Bobby Grant.

With no job, the bills began to mount – not that you'd have thought so from the way Tracy and Doreen behaved. Grounded and bored, Tracy resorted to Chatline and clocked up a huge bill while dozy Doe thought a new credit card would see them through their financial problems. With an airhead for a wife and for a daughter, Billy had a lot to put up with.

And for good measure, there was always his younger brother Jimmy. In any other family, Jimmy would have been the black sheep but with the Corkhills, he blended in perfectly. Dumping a pile of 'hot' bricks on Billy's drive, he announced that they were to build a nice new garage. In view of the criminal activity surrounding the family, it was perhaps not altogether surprising that Billy disapproved of Rod's plans to join the force. It was like being a traitor to the family name.

In the summer of 1986, Billy was approached by Julian Tyler, an aggressive businessman with no time for trade unions. He offered Billy a job as maintenance supervisor. Branded a scab, Billy knew that work would be hard to find so he gave it a go. Besides, the money was good. The only drawback was the bleeper which Billy was obliged to carry around at all times. He was expected to be on call night and day. It drove him mad. In the end, he committed the cardinal sin of smashing his bleeper. When Tyler came round to remonstrate, Doreen told him he could keep his rotten job.

After a brief stint as a model (she seemed to forget that models are required to smile), Tracy signed up for a YTS hairdressing scheme. She wasted no time in getting on the wrong side of the salon owner, Shelley Rimmer. Within four months, she had been sacked for being rude. Most customers would have preferred to have had their hair cut by Sweeney Todd.

'C'mon, c'mon, I'm only a doleite! Who else wants to crap on me? C'mon. C'mon, eh? You can have me wife for a fiver if you want. C'mon, I'm only a doley. Drive over me lawn. C'mon, drive over me bloody lawn. It doesn't matter, I'm only a doleite.'

– Billy Corkhill, driving manically over everyone's lawns

Things were desperate at number 10. The phone and the electricity had been cut off and the TV repossessed. The Corkhills were

Rod arrests a dangerous-looking shoplifter.

listed as bad payers. But Doreen was still a good spender. So when Billy was offered work in Tunbridge Wells, he had no choice but to accept it. His spell down south solved nothing. When he came back two months later, the bills were still waiting to be paid. He was beside himself with worry. The house became a tip. A brick through the window would have been classified as home improvement.

The only member of the family who appeared to be coping was Rod. He went off to Police College, still fearful, however, that some Corkhill skeleton would one day wreck his chances of joining the force. With Uncle Jimmy an increasingly frequent visitor, he had good cause for concern. Jimmy's solution to the family's debts was to suggest a fake burglary, followed by a hefty insurance claim. For added authenticity, after breaking into number 10, Jimmy popped across the road and turned over the Collinses'. That wasn't part of the deal. Jimmy, as usual, had gone too far. Billy insisted that Jimmy retrieve a brooch which had sentimental value for Annabelle and he carefully placed it down the side of the Collinses' sofa so that they would find it. Billy was not about to start robbing his neighbours.

For an electrician, Billy's fuse was growing worryingly short. To avoid the hole in the road, Pat Hancock drove his van over Billy's garden. Billy rushed out to thump him but somebody had already beaten him to it. Pat had a smashed nose following a repossession job. Billy then parked his car across the drive to prevent anyone else abusing his property. Soon the Corkhills found themselves facing repossession proceedings. The spendthrift Doreen hid the letter from Billy but confided in her dentist boss, Mr Howman. He offered to lend her money and heavily hinted that she could repay him with her body. Doreen was in a quandary. Telling Billy it was a staff dinner, she went alone to a hotel with Howman and after the meal, headed up to his room. Once there, she realised she'd need an anaesthetic to go through with it and ran out, telling Howman where he could stick his money. Back home, she finally showed Billy the letter from the building society. Billy took out his frustration by driving over the neighbours' lawns. Harry Cross called round to complain about the mess Billy had made but wisely backed off when he saw Billy's mood. It was not often Harry shied away from a battle . . .

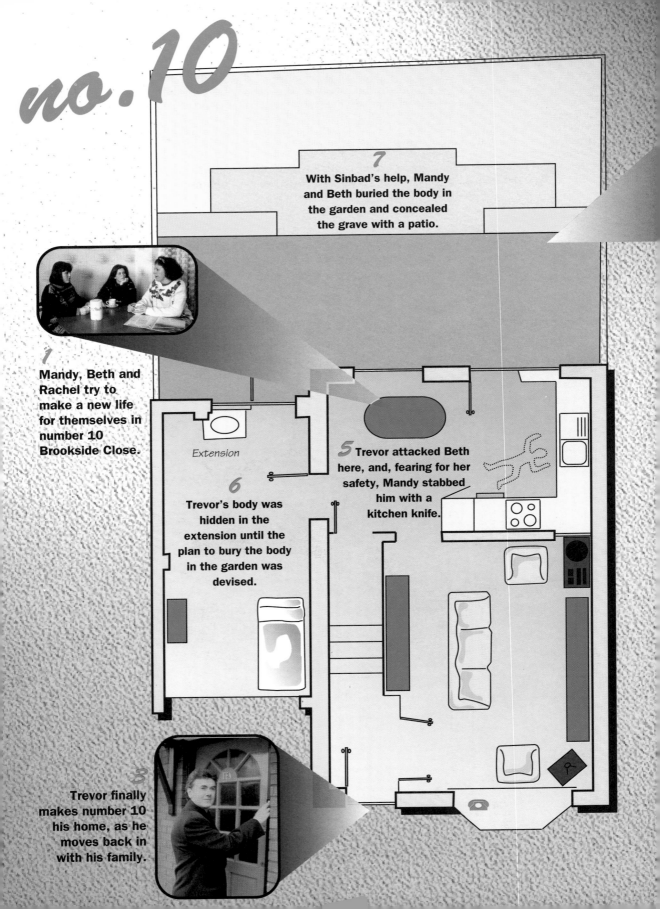

no.10

7 With Sinbad's help, Mandy and Beth buried the body in the garden and concealed the grave with a patio.

1 Mandy, Beth and Rachel try to make a new life for themselves in number 10 Brookside Close.

5 Trevor attacked Beth here, and, fearing for her safety, Mandy stabbed him with a kitchen knife.

Extension

6 Trevor's body was hidden in the extension until the plan to bury the body in the garden was devised.

3 Trevor finally makes number 10 his home, as he moves back in with his family.

The Jordache Family

2
Trevor, locked out in the rain. At first, Mandy stood her ground and would not let him back into the family.

In 1993 number 10 became a safe house, and in March of that year Mandy Jordache moved in, in an attempt to escape her brutal husband, Trevor. With her daughters Beth and Rachel, she hoped to start a new life in safety.

One of the most dramatic storylines ever seen in Brookside Close began when Trevor managed to track his family down. No one knew why Mandy didn't want to see her husband. He seemed so charming at first. It was only when he moved back in with Mandy, Beth and Rachel that the truth came out: Trevor was a violent man who abused his wife and elder daughter. When Trevor attacked Beth in the midst of a bitter argument, Mandy stabbed him and the terrified mother and daughter buried him in the garden. The resourceful Sinbad proceeded to camouflage the grave with a patio.

upstairs

Beth's room

Rachel's room

Mandy's room

4
Trevor begins to terrorise his wife soon after moving in. Mandy and Beth managed to hide the truth about him from Rachel.

Billy turned to crime. Asking Jimmy to use his underworld contacts, he landed a nice little earner as getaway driver on a supermarket raid for a local villain named Gene. At the reception following Jonathan and Laura's wedding, Billy frantically chatted to as many people as possible in an attempt to establish an alibi. Then he nipped out of the marquee to join the rest of the gang.

The robbery went horribly wrong. Unable to prise the case from the supermarket manager, the gang were forced to bundle him into the back seat of the car. The rest were wearing balaclavas but Billy's face was unmasked. The manager had a perfect view of him and even knew his name after Gene had carelessly ordered 'Billy' to drive off. As Billy hared through the streets, the gang abandoned their attempt to get at the money and ran off, leaving Billy with the manager who was bleeding profusely from a stab wound. Billy wanted to run off too but couldn't leave the bloke to die. So he dumped him at the nearest hospital.

Billy was sure it was only a matter of time before the police picked him up. Whenever a car pulled onto the Close, he expected it to have a blue light. Gene thought so too and, to ensure Billy's silence, he mugged Tracy. She knew something was amiss when she later spotted Billy with Gene. Doreen was also highly suspicious. She was not sleeping at night and said that unless he told her everything, she would leave him. So Billy revealed the whole sorry episode. Doreen was bitter. Not unreasonably, she thought having a convicted armed robber for a father might jeopardise Rod's career prospects. Then she told him her little secret – about

Billy acts as getaway driver for Gene on the supermarket robbery. As with all of Billy's get-rich-quick schemes, it went horribly wrong.

Howman – and said she now wished she had slept with him. Billy slapped her. Doreen walked out. Later, Rod returned home and proudly announced that there was only the robbers' driver to pick up now. That was all Billy needed to hear.

In keeping with the mood in the Corkhills' house, Tracy and her wastrel boyfriend Jamie Henderson painted her bedroom black. Gene, showing little regard for the maxim 'honour amongst thieves', incriminated Billy and he was taken in for questioning. There was to be an identity parade. Rod, who had been sent home, was confident that his dad would now be released. Billy's heart sank. Yet the supermarket manager, Riordan, failed to pick him out. Billy was indeed free to go. But he was not free from Riordan. A few weeks later, he paid Billy a visit. Riordan was by no means as pure as the Fairy Snow and tried to blackmail Billy into robbing his supermarket for him. Doreen overheard the conversation and vowed that if Billy had anything to do with the scheme, she would leave him for good. That in itself must have seemed a tempting offer.

Billy felt he had no choice but to go along with Riordan. When Riordan wanted more, Billy called his bluff and Riordan backed off. But as far as Doreen was concerned, it was too late. She had carried out her threat and gone to stay with her mother. Billy was confident that she would soon be back.

It soon became apparent that Doe would not be coming home. Billy felt aggrieved – after all, it was partly her spending spree that landed him in bother in the first place. Nevertheless, he wanted her back, just so that they could be one big miserable family again. He had heard she was in Bristol but his visit there proved fruitless.

In the early part of 1988, Billy began to take in more waifs and strays than the RSPCA. Jamie, who was forever being kicked out of his own home and who had spent some weeks hiding in the Corkhills' garage, moved in on a steadier footing and was joined by Jimmy and his mistress, Sheila Grant's best friend Kathy Roach. Jimmy was still married to Jackie. They had met back in 1971. He had noticed her in a pub, wearing tight white jeans, and, on their second date, bought her *Never Ending Song of Love* by the New Seekers. In spite of this, they continued seeing each other and were subsequently married. They had a daughter, Lindsey, and a son, Jimmy junior, but eventually Jimmy's womanising ways resulted in Jackie throwing him out. Jimmy junior never forgave his father for finding him in bed with Jackie's sister Val, when the boy was just eight. Kathy had also been kicked out by her husband and so followed Jimmy to Brookside Close. Her principal recommendation appeared to be that she worked for a bookmaker. It was Jimmy's ideal combination – sex and the 2.30 at Lingfield. Jimmy usually finished before his horse.

Jimmy made himself useful by building an extension to the house and it soon came in handy when another homeless soul turned up on Billy's doorstep. It was Sheila Grant, fresh from her split with Bobby. Kathy had persuaded Billy to put Sheila and her three-year-old daughter Claire up for a while. Billy always was a soft touch.

Back in work and with the threat of criminal proceedings now a distant memory, Billy began to relax. He dated Linda, a woman from work, and made Sheila welcome at home. This was, of course, more than Tracy did. She wanted her mum back and bitterly resented Sheila's presence. Tracy's state of mind was further complicated by problems at work. She was back on the hairdressing scene but was being sexually harassed by the manager, Gerrard. When she refused to co-operate, he sacked her. Acting on Sheila's advice, Tracy took him to an industrial tribunal. She won £1,500 damages and her job. On her first day back at the salon, she heard one of Gerrard's former customers complaining about his dismissal. In true Tracy fashion, she reacted by spraying the woman's face with hot

water. She offered to resign but the new manager, Antony, insisted that she stayed. Where else would he find an act like Tracy?

Meanwhile, Rod had been struck down with a nagging pain – his girlfriend, Kirsty Brown. A nurse at the local hospital, Kirsty was a killjoy of the first order. Rod was supposed to be saving up for their future and was not allowed to spend any money without her say-so. His mates at the station, notably PC Neil 'Tommo' Thompson, ribbed him that he had thumb prints on his head. Rod decided he was too young to die and, to inject a little excitement into his life, asked sexy WPC Emma Reid to accompany him to her bedroom. When Kirsty saw the scratch marks, he had a lot of explaining to do and was forced to make a statement to the effect that he wanted to marry her. But when Kirsty spotted Rod and Emma together on his 21st birthday outing to Blackpool, she called off the engagement. For Rod, it was a close shave.

Against this background of turmoil, Billy and Sheila grew closer. It was an unlikely friendship – the straight-laced Catholic and the armed robber. Perhaps Sheila saw something of Barry in Billy. But before she could even consider anything more than friendship with Billy, she had to wrestle with her conscience. Big Daddy could not have given her a stiffer fight. She consulted a priest who reminded her that she was still married to Bobby.

Christmas 1988 brought Sheila the best present ever – a surprise visit from Damon's girlfriend, Debbie, just over a year after his death. And she was holding his son and Sheila's grandson, Simon. She hadn't had an abortion after all. Sheila was overjoyed. She had always liked Debbie. In an emotional reunion, they talked about their past and of their hopes for the future. Billy gave Sheila and Claire a rosary each and admitted that he no longer wanted Doreen back. Sheila and Billy cemented their new relationship with a New Year's kiss.

Barry, jealous of any man who came between him and his mam, did his best to wreck things. He suggested Sheila move permanently to Basingstoke where her sister, Margaret Jefferson, lived. Sheila did spend a few days down there but her sister told her to find happiness – in spite of her religion, if necessary. She returned to Billy's arms and Billy's bed. Barry stumbled across them and made no attempt to conceal his disapproval. Barry was not the only one trying to split up the happy couple. Julia had constantly attempted to unsettle Sheila by telling her that Doreen would be back soon but so far none of the rumours had

Rod goes undercover in the amusement arcade to investigate the activities of rent-boy Craig.

upholding the family tradition), he left Godden stranded outside a nightclub following an armed robbery . . . and with the club's bouncers closing in fast.

Following an unsuccessful attempt to win back Kirsty (she had been dating his mate Tommo), Rod took up with Diana Spence, a young pharmacy assistant who had served him with spot cream while he was on undercover work. He had told her he was a trainee supermarket manager and when she discovered the truth, neither she nor her father were amused. It emerged that Diana's mum had run off with a copper.

Diana was a pleasant girl, if a little slow on the uptake. She eventually revealed that she was illiterate. Again Rod, Brookside's answer to Poirot, had failed to detect any signs.

Having been sacked from the salon for touting for business, Tracy set up on her own. In May 1991, her pal Nikki and Rod's mate Tommo moved into number 10 and Tracy found herself in the middle of a tug of love between the ever-present Barry and a sharp young policeman, Mark Potter. When Mark tried to rape her, Tracy defended herself by stabbing him in the arm with a pair of hairdressing scissors.

Rod was all set to marry Diana in December 1991. He had been unofficially frequenting an amusement arcade where he had earlier been on undercover surveillance. His interest was a rent boy, Craig, whom Rod wanted to free from the clutches of his pimp. On the day of his wedding, disobeying orders, he followed Craig to the toilets of Lime Street Station. Eddie the pimp was waiting. Rod was beaten up and spent the afternoon in hospital instead of church. Rod was suspended from the force. It was the beginning of the end of his love affair with the police. He and Diana finally managed a Register Office wedding in the summer of 1992 but a month later, her worst fears about her husband's job were realised when Rod was slashed with a knife during a raid on the hair salon on Brookside Parade. She persuaded him to quit the force for good and he took a security job in Warrington.

Since attending illiteracy classes, Diana had been growing in confidence. She became less reliant on Rod and found that she had more in common with the sympathetic Peter Harrison. After just three months of marriage, she and Rod argued bitterly over her friendship with Peter. Rod lost control, slapped her and walked out.

The house was up for sale. A couple called the Shackletons inspected it closely before buying. A few weeks before Christmas 1992, Diana moved out of number 10 and into the Farnhams' on a temporary basis, pending the rape trial. Rod came back briefly for the trial but left as soon as the not guilty verdict was announced. This just confirmed to him she'd been a willing partner in the affair. A distraught Diana later tried to take her own life by slashing her wrists. Peter attempted to comfort her but she told him she never wanted to see him again. Even though the jury hadn't believed her story, she knew that Peter had raped her.

She had a short stint working at the local nightclub, La Luz, but was unable to cope with the attention of a group of rowdy men. She reacted by throwing a glass of lager in the face of one of them. It was not exactly the image the club wanted from its staff.

The new occupants of 10 Brookside Close were shrouded in a veil of secrecy, a nervous twitch of the curtains, a hesitant half-opening of the door. They were not the Shackletons at all but the Jordaches – Mandy and her teenage daughters Beth and Rachel. Mrs Shackleton had bought the house for them, and others in a similar situation, to live in. For, somewhat ironically in view of its history, number 10 had become a 'safe house', a refuge for battered women. How anybody or anything could be deemed safe on Brookside Close is something of a mystery.

Mandy's biggest mistake in life had been marrying Trevor, a silver-tongued Irishman who abused both herself and Beth. With Trevor in prison, the family were rehoused in the Close to start afresh. Mandy told the neighbours that her husband was dead but he soon returned to haunt them.

'I really have changed, you know, and I will never lay a finger on you again.'
– Trevor Jordache to Mandy

It did not take Trevor long to track them down after his parole. At first, he appeared all sweetness and light, promising that he was a different man. Weak-willed Mandy was taken in by him, disregarding the views of Beth who didn't want him anywhere near the house. When Mandy allowed Trevor to stay for a couple of nights, Beth moved into the Harrisons'. She couldn't bear to be under the same roof as him after what he had done. The scheming Trevor gradually worked his way back in on a more permanent basis. Once he had achieved that aim, the drinking and the beatings started all over again. He crept into Rachel's bed and back into Mandy's, threatening her that if she told anybody about his past misdemeanours, he would kill her, the girls and then himself.

On 7 May 1993, he was spared the trouble. During the course of another brutal assault after discovering that he was being poisoned with weedkiller and tablets, Trevor lashed out at Beth in the kitchen, the scene of so many rows between Billy and Doe. Fearing for both her and her daughter's life, Mandy seized a kitchen knife from a cupboard and plunged it into his back. Their evil tormentor was dead at last.

Telling Rachel that Trevor was slumped on the floor in a drunken sleep, Mandy and Beth set about covering their tracks. They passed off the stench of the corpse as blocked drains and bought a consignment of air freshener to underline the point. Mentally, Beth was the stronger of the two. She wrapped the body in binbags and dragged it into the extension with a little help from Mandy. Borrowing a spade from Peter, Beth started to bury her father in the back garden. Mandy looked on as the husband she once loved disappeared under a mound of soil.

Sinbad, who had become friendly with Mandy, realised something was afoot. He had found the knife and, observing the pile of earth and listening to Rachel's dismay that daddy had gone away, concluded that Trevor was no longer in the land of the living. He never said as much to Mandy or Beth but instead offered to build a patio over the newly-dug soil. Mandy readily agreed. The message between them was understood.

But the Jordaches' troubles were far from over. Trevor's nosey sister Brenna saw to that. She refused to believe that Trevor had just disappeared and notified the police. Brenna saw Trevor as a saint and was of the opinion that Mandy had provoked him into his past violence. Mandy knew that Brenna would never give up so when the police announced that a body had been found – and that it might be Trevor – it seemed like a heaven-sent opportunity to bury Trevor once and for all. The body was unrecognisable through decomposition but Mandy identified the belongings as being Trevor's. It was, of course, somebody else altogether.

As Rachel and Brenna came to terms with Trevor's death, Brenna made one last request. She would like her brother's signet ring – the one that was buried with the real Trevor in the garden. So during Beth's 18th birthday party at La Luz, Sinbad dug up the body and retrieved the ring.

There were other scares. At one point, the Bankses were on the verge of buying the house – and its grisly secret – and then Roy Williams, a sinister cellmate of Trevor's, turned up and started blackmailing Mandy. Afraid that he knew something, she coughed up £700 – from the money Sinbad had collected for the Tony Dixon fund. To pay back the money, Sinbad visited a loan shark. The loan was subsequently taken over by the shifty Kenny Maguire who immediately announced that the repayments had gone up.

By now a fully-fledged medical student at Liverpool University, Beth recovered from her aborted romance with Peter Harrison by developing a close friendship with Margaret Clemence. At first, it was nothing more than that but Beth slowly

Trevor's old cell-mate, Roy Williams, takes Sinbad's breath away.

realised that her feelings for Margaret were more than just friendship. She craved any form of physical contact with Margaret – their girlie cuddles grew longer and closer – and missed her like mad when she wasn't around. Beth broke the news to Margaret with a passionate kiss. Margaret backed away to Oldham, feeling awkward and confused. To convince herself that she was not a lesbian, Margaret jumped into bed with Keith Rooney at the first opportunity. But deep down, she felt okay about kissing Beth. After a night out, they went back to the Farnhams' (Max and Patricia were away in Oxford). Margaret told Beth she could sleep in Thomas's room but, unable to sleep herself, Margaret crept into Beth's bed and asked Beth to hold her. They dozed off in each other's arms.

In the cold light of day, Margaret was less sure. And when Beth was pursued by Chris, a 30-year-old gay university lecturer, Margaret had seen enough. She realised that she still missed Derek. She phoned him up and, to her delight, he asked her to come out to Bosnia where he was now working. Before you could say Beth Jordache, Margaret was on the next flight out.

Beth and Chris flung themselves into an affair. They managed to keep it secret

*After Margaret, Beth fell for
her lecturer, Chris.*

until Rachel spotted them cuddling on a day trip to New Brighton and then David Crosbie caught them playing tonsil hockey at the Farnhams'. When Mandy found out, Beth moved into Chris's flat. But after Mandy had threatened to report Chris to the education authorities, Chris dropped Beth like a hot potato. So Beth was obliged to troop back to number 10 while Mandy tried to adjust to having a lesbian daughter.

Sinbad was very fond of Mandy but, understandably enough, she repeatedly shied away from a relationship. But when his mother, Ruth, who had been staying in the extension after being taken ill, revealed that he had an uncle Jake in Australia and

that they were both invited out there, Sinbad was sorely tempted to emigrate. He got as far as handing in his notice as caretaker at Brookside Parade before Mandy finally declared her true feelings for him. He worked hard on Mandy and elicited considerable sympathy after straining his back repairing the windows following the explosion at number 5. Nevertheless, Mandy was still not prepared to make a firm commitment. But Sinbad would not be put off. They'd been through too much together. Happiness and 10 Brookside Close had always been strange bedfellows.

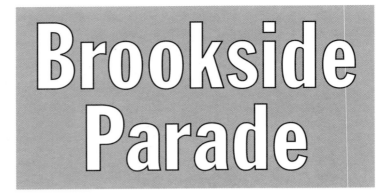

Brookside Parade

'*She was too close to the edge. I grabbed her arm. She had a look on her face – that scared look. The silly cow got her foot caught. I put me hand out to catch her – well, I think that's what I did – I was so flaming angry with her. I mean, in me head, in my head, I know I put me hand out to save them. I know what I did, but in me dreams, I remember thinking, I could hurt her. I could do it now. I could make her pay for everything she's done.*'

– Barry Grant to Terry

Even in construction, the Brookside Parade of shops maintained the corpse count of the nearby Close. On 4 October 1991, Sue and Danny Sullivan plunged to their deaths from the top of the adjacent scaffolding. The besotted Graeme Curtis, who had turned up at Sue's house that morning with a bouquet of flowers, was convicted of the murders. However Sue's workmate, Fran Pearson, another to be impregnated by Sheila's boy, uncovered the truth. Barry, seized with a sudden surge of honesty after belatedly finding out that Matty Nolan was his real father, decided to tell Terry before Fran did. On a deserted beach, he took Terry through old times and more recent ones. Terry, on a rare sober day in the wake of the trial, didn't want to know and began to walk away. But Barry wasn't finished. He produced a shotgun and fired a shot which flew past Terry's shoulder. Sure of his buddy's attention, he yelled out: 'I slept with Sue. I 'ad her on your settee.' Terry exploded. 'Everything I had, you always had to ruin.' He had a point.

There was more. Barry recounted the events of the fateful day on the scaffolding before handing over the gun to Terry and saying: 'Do your own justice.' But Terry thought that was too easy a way out for

Gunfight on Southport beach. Barry challenges Terry to avenge the deaths of Sue and Danny.

Mick, Ellis, Matty and Mike stage a quiet opening for Pizza Parade.

Barry. He wanted Barry to suffer for the rest of his life. With no sign of Barry, just a lot of blood, Terry was hauled in for suspected murder by DS Kent. Then the charge might have stuck had Barry not ambled in to the station, wondering what all the fuss was about.

With the money from the sale of number 9, Terry had opened a shop called Pizza Parade. It was soon clear that Terry and pizzas were no more compatible than steak and custard, besides which he had the business brain of the average moose. Any profits, he drank. At one stage, the health department closed the shop down on the grounds of food poisoning. Terry became more of a sleeping partner and sold out to Mick and Ellis Johnson who livened the place up by getting Keith Rooney to paint some fancy artwork on the pavement outside the door. Mick eventually settled in the flat above the shop with Marianne Dwyer, who, on the eve of her proposed wedding to Ellis, realised she was about to marry the wrong brother. Downstairs, Mick received help from the pushy Carol Salter. Carol had more on her mind than cheesy topping but Mick made it clear that he wasn't for sale.

When Carol went into hospital, her unruly teenage son Garry moved in with Mick and Marianne. Mick became some-thing of a second father to the lad, much to the annoyance of Marianne and Garry's real dad who suddenly appeared on the scene after being released from prison. For a while, it was pizza with menaces.

Terry, meanwhile, had also obtained a flat above the shops, by way of a favour from Barry in return for a guarantee of silence. There he courted Anna Wolska whom he was prepared to marry but she could not go through with it. She liked him too much! Instead Barry, fretting over the fact that Fran had fled to Greece with Stephen, the son he had once kidnapped, made Anna an alternative offer. He would marry her if she'd have his baby. Anna agreed but when she found out more about Barry's past, she went off the idea. Barry wanted his money back. She tried to elope with Terry but an angry Barry shopped her to the immigration authorities. Barry had done it again!

Terry was later installed as manager of the petrol station, with Bible-bashing Simon Howe as his assistant. Terry saw the light. It was the only garage where they gave away

Garage owner George Webb gets a taste of his own medicine.

Brookside Parade

La Luz (first floor)

Pizza Parade

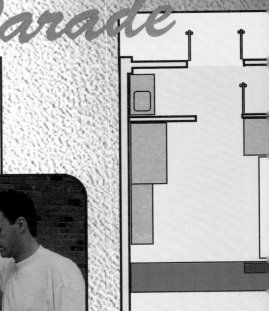

1
Sue and Danny were pushed from the top of the scaffolding alongside what is now La Luz.

2
Barry Grant was always hanging around the shops, inspecting his new acquisition.

3
Terry was unable to account for his movements on the fatal day.

4
Terry attacked the other suspect, Graeme Curtis, at Sue and Danny's funeral. Curtis was later found guilty of committing the double murder.

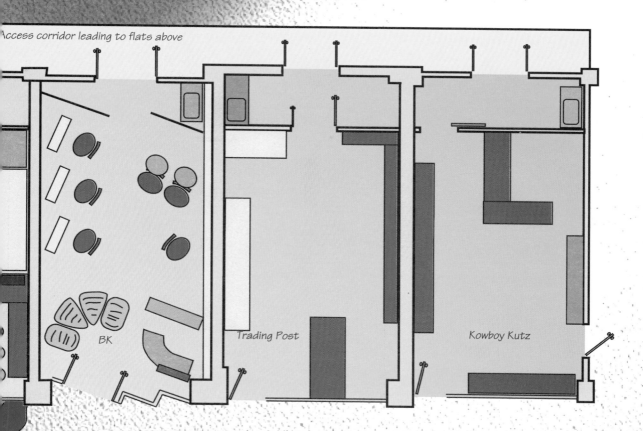

BK

Trading Post

Kowboy Kutz

The Murders of Sue and Danny Sullivan

There were more suspects for the murders of Sue and Danny Sullivan than there had been on the Orient Express. Was it Graeme Curtis, the work colleague who had been hopelessly infatuated with Sue? Or her husband, Terry, who had recently found out that he was not Danny's real father? Or Terry's pal, Barry Grant, who threatened Sue and slept with her depending on how the mood took him?

That morning in October 1991, Graeme had called on Sue at home and insisted that he talk to her. They arranged a rendezvous outside the Brookside Shopping Parade, then under construction. While her back was turned, little Danny scaled the scaffolding before you could say 'Chris Bonington'. Sue went up to rescue Danny but she and her son plunged to their deaths following an altercation with a mystery man. Graeme Curtis was convicted of the murders (he subsequently took his own life) but the true culprit was Barry although he claimed it was all an accident. Then he would, wouldn't he?

Jackie Corkhill tries to find out whether Ron is past his sell-by date.

Rod Corkhill is attacked during the raid on Angela Lambert's hair salon.

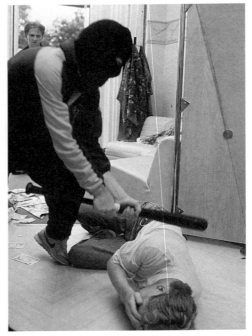

Bibles instead of glasses. After the explosion on the Close, Terry and Simon shared Barry's flat, to the fury of Mr Grant who thought he had finally got Simon out of his life. Terry had taken over the garage from George Webb, the racist thug who had made the Johnsons' life a nightmare. Webb tried to win over Ron Dixon after hearing daughter Jacqui say that he had objected to her going out with Keith because of Keith's colour. Webb's campaign to get rid of the Johnsons began with stickers bearing the slogan 'Strength Through Purity' being placed on the pizza parlour window. He graduated to graffiti and petrol bombs. Fortunately, before Webb could carry out that final horrific threat, Ron Dixon came to his senses and stopped him bombing the Johnsons' bungalow.

Next door to Ron's Trading Post, Jimmy Corkhill saw Barry Grant's absence as an opportunity to squat. So without paying any rent, he opened up Kowboy Kutz, a cheapo emporium designed to undercut Ron Dixon. Ron complained to the estate agents, Fletcher's, where Max Farnham worked but old Maxie was powerless to act since Jimmy hadn't done any criminal damage to the shop. Even with his water and electricity cut off, Jimmy was determined to stay put. When he returned from Spain, Barry had a more practical solution. He set fire to the place, unaware that Jimmy had installed gas

cylinders. As Barry dialled 999 from the nearby phone, the front of the shop was blown out. Jimmy took the hint.

That Christmas Derek O'Farrell then took over the unit as a charity shop before DD Dixon turned it into a florist's. Jean Crosbie later helped out and Patricia Farnham had her PR office above the shop.

After the Trading Post, the second unit to be opened was a hairdressing salon run by the attractive Angela Lambert, who was separated from her husband Colin. Needless to say, Barry also took a keen interest in Angela's welfare but, after initial enthusiasm, the cool Angela had the measure of him. She quit the salon in September 1992 after the robbery and Brian Kennedy took over as franchise owner. With Tracy Corkhill as stylist and Julia Brogan sweeping up, it was a wonder he had any customers. Brian seemed a decent chap – Tracy certainly thought so – but he had a secret vice, drugs. And he wanted Jimmy Corkhill to provide them.

Jimmy was working at La Luz, the night-club separated from Pizza Parade by an alleyway. Barry Grant was co-owner of this trendy new night scene, which opened on Christmas Day 1992 with a Spanish fiesta theme. While Barry celebrated the opening night, he was blissfully unaware that Terry was upstairs in his flat with Fran and Barry's son Stephen. Barry's first partner at

Opening night at La Luz.

the club was Joe Halsall, a tough little lady who, as head of Halsall Leisure, introduced Anna Wolska to life as an escort agent. Barry and Joe were soon at loggerheads over his plans to hold raves at the club. She tried to buy him out but, through Max, Barry met the eccentric Oscar Dean who discovered that Joe had been cooking the books. Barry threatened to torch the club – a party trick of his, as he revealed to a stunned Jimmy – but Joe countered by framing him for a hit and run on Jimmy. It was Oscar who bailed Barry out by persuading Jimmy to withdraw his incriminating statement. To the frustration of the promoted DI Kent, Barry was released from prison. He returned to La Luz to find Oscar sitting behind the desk. Exit Joe, enter Oscar.

'It looks like that's where you're headed. Prison, Jimmy. And if it gets you off this rubbish, it'll be the best thing for you.'
– Jackie Corkhill

Oscar offered Barry a 60/40 partnership in the club. Barry gratefully accepted. Oscar's vision for La Luz was somewhere cheap and cheerful and packed every night but it soon became a drug haven. When a horrified Jimmy spotted dealers in operation, Oscar strongly advised him to turn a blind eye. Joe may have had her faults but she didn't encourage drug-taking in the club. Jimmy relayed his findings to Brian Kennedy but Brian had a different view of drugs and told Jimmy that he couldn't argue against something he'd never tried. To prove himself to Brian, Jimmy took one of the Ecstasy tabs he had confiscated from the punters.

Tempted by the prospect of ready cash, Jimmy was soon in Brian's employ, supplying him with drugs to order. Jimmy envied Brian's lifestyle and enjoyed being part of his scene, even though in reality, he was nothing more than a gopher. So when Brian offered him the opportunity to cut in on a big deal, Jimmy jumped at the chance. He thought the money would impress Jackie with whom he had finally been reunited. He wanted to buy her their dream house. Brian told him the deal had gone well but instead of cash, the cokehead coiffeur handed Jimmy a jiffy bag containing £3,000 worth of cocaine. Jimmy protested but Brian told him to get it stashed quickly and keep his head down.

Restless, he waited for news then saw Brian Kennedy being escorted from the salon by the police. Jimmy didn't have time to say goodbye to Brian but he had just said goodbye to £3,000 cash. All he had was the coke.

Lying low for a while, Jimmy sampled some of his stash. He soon found that the only way he could get through the day was by taking drugs. He was sure he'd got it under control, even after he'd caused the deaths of Frank Rogers and Tony Dixon. He moved on to harder stuff. There was more cold turkey than on Boxing Day at Bernard Matthews'. Jackie stoically stood by him, desperately trying to cure him. Jimmy made promises but broke them even quicker. To finance his need for drugs, he turned to burglary. Then Eddie Banks caught him in the act. Jimmy was sentenced to nine months in prison. Inside, he discovered he'd been a mug as a druggie – there were easier ways to make money: as a drug dealer . . .

Drug-crazed Jimmy Corkhill.

Brookside Parade

The Explosion at Kowboy Kutz

With the shop next door the Trading Post standing empty, the entrepreneurial Jimmy Corkhill decided to squat and open up his own business. He called it Kowboy Kutz, a shrine to the knocked-off. Barry Grant was in Spain at the time and so Jimmy was able to continue his illegal occupation without paying any rent. Ron Dixon, who saw his own trade suffering, was particularly irate. Barry's return brought a swift end to affairs. Unable to evict Jimmy, he resorted to his own brand of diplomacy and set fire to the place. Alas, he was unaware that Jimmy had installed gas cylinders and the front of the shop was blown out. Barry's eyebrows may have been singed but his reputation wasn't, and Jimmy didn't even have time to arrange a sale of damaged stock.

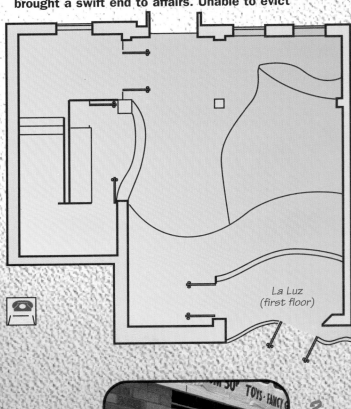

La Luz
(first floor)

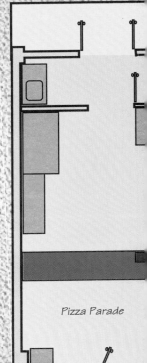

Pizza Parade

2

Barry Grant left the scene to summon the fire brigade from a nearby pay-phone. His call was rudely interrupted by the blast.